BLAKE'S

Maths Guide

for Middle primary students

Bev Dunbar

PASCAL PRESS

Blake's Maths Guide
Middle Primary

Copyright © 2011 Blake Education and Bev Dunbar
Reprinted 2012, 2014, 2015, 2016, 2018

ISBN: 978 1 74215 903 4

Published by Pascal Press
PO Box 250
Glebe NSW 2037
www.pascalpress.com.au
contact@pascalpress.com.au

Author: Bev Dunbar
Publisher: Lynn Dickinson
Edited by Karen Jayne
Design and illustration by Janice Bowles
Typeset by Julian Mole, Post Pre-press Group
Printed by Vivar Printing/Green Giant Press

CONTENTS

NUMBER and ALGEBRA	ELABORATIONS	ACMNA	PAGE
Number and place value			
Investigate the conditions required for a number to be odd or even and identify odd and even numbers	★ Skip count by 2s, group objects in 2s ★ Explain why numbers ending in 0, 2, 4, 6, 8 are even and numbers ending in 1, 3, 5, 7, 9 are odd	51	1 1–2
Recognise, model, represent and order numbers to at least 10 000	★ Place four-digit numbers on a number line ★ Write numbers as words	52	3–9
Apply place value to partition, rearrange and regroup numbers to at least 10 000 to assist calculations and solve problems	★ Recognise 10 000 equals 10 thousands, 100 hundreds, 1000 tens and 10 000 ones	53	3–9
Recall addition facts for single-digit numbers and related subtraction facts to develop increasingly efficient mental strategies for computation	★ Use quick recall facts to solve addition and subtraction problems with larger numbers	54, 55	10–11, 13–16
Recall multiplication facts of two, three, five and ten and related division facts	★ Establish number facts using number sequences	56	18–33
Represent and solve problems involving multiplication using efficient mental and written strategies and appropriate digital technologies	★ Write simple word problems in numerical form	57	18–33
Fractions and decimals			
Model and represent unit fractions including 1/2, 1/4, 1/3, 1/5 and their multiples to a complete whole	★ Locate unit fractions on a number line ★ Partition lengths, areas and collections to create halves, thirds, quarters, fifths	58	35–40
Money and financial mathematics			
Represent money values in multiple ways and count the change required for simple transactions to the nearest five cents	★ Recognise the relationship between dollars and cents	59	44–48
Patterns and algebra			
Describe, continue, and create number patterns resulting from performing addition or subtraction	★ Identify, describe and write rules for number patterns	60	49–53
MEASUREMENT and GEOMETRY		ACMMG	
Using units of measurement			
Measure, order and compare objects with familiar metric units of length, mass and capacity	★ Recognise and use centimetres and metres, grams and kilograms, and millilitres and litres	61	54–61, 70–72, 75–77
Tell time to the minute and investigate the relationship between units of time	★ Recognise that there are 60 minutes in an hour and 60 seconds in a minute	62	81–84
Shape			
Make models of three-dimensional objects and describe key features	★ Explore 3D objects such as prisms and pyramids	63	97–111
Location and transformation			
Create and interpret simple grid maps to show position and pathways	★ Create a map of the classroom or playground	65	138–139
Identify symmetry in the environment	★ Identify symmetry in art, and the natural and built environment	66	123–125
Geometric reasoning			
Identify angles as measures of turn and compare angle sizes in everyday situations	★ Recognise analogue clocks use angles to indicate time ★ Open doors, partially and fully, and compare size of angles created	64	125, 137 126–129

© Australian Curriculum, Assessment and Reporting Authority 2010.

STATISTICS and PROBABILITY		ACMSP	
Chance			
Conduct chance experiments, identify and describe possible outcomes and recognise variation in results	★ Conduct repeated trials of chance experiments and identify variations between trials	67	146–149
Data representation and interpretation			
Identify questions or issues for categorical variables. Identify data sources and plan methods of data collection and recording	★ Refine questions, and plan and carry out investigations to collect data	68	151–152
Collect data, organise into categories and create displays using lists, tables, picture graphs and simple column graphs, with and without the use of digital technologies	★ Explore efficient ways to record data, represent and report results of investigations	69	153–159
Interpret and compare data displays	★ Compare and describe similarities and differences	70	153–159

AUSTRALIAN CURRICULUM CORRELATIONS – YEAR 4

NUMBER and ALGEBRA	ELABORATIONS	ACMNA	PAGE
Number and place value			
Investigate and use the properties of odd and even numbers	★ Use four operations with pairs of odd and even numbers	71	2
Recognise, represent and order numbers to at least tens of thousands	★ Reproduce five-digit numbers in words	72	8–9
Apply place value to partition, rearrange and regroup numbers to at least tens of thousands to assist calculations and solve problems	★ Recognise that the place-value pattern is built on multiplication and division	73	3–9
Investigate number sequences involving multiples of 3, 4, 6, 7, 8, and 9	★ Recognise that number sequences can be extended indefinitely and determine any patterns in the sequences	74	18–25, 28–33
Recall multiplication facts up to 10 × 10 and related division facts	★ Use known multiplication facts to calculate related division facts	75	26–27
Develop efficient mental and written strategies and use appropriate digital technologies for multiplication and for division where there is no remainder	★ Use strategies such as commutativity, doubling, halving	76	12, 16–17
Fractions and decimals			
Investigate equivalent fractions used in context	★ Explore relationships between families of fractions (halves/quarters/eighths, thirds/sixths)	77	35–40
Count by quarters, halves and thirds, including with mixed numerals. Locate and represent these fractions on a number line	★ Convert mixed numbers to improper fractions	78	35–40
Recognise that the place value system can be extended to tenths and hundredths. Make connections between fractions and decimal notation	★ Use division by 10 to extend the place-value system ★ Establish equivalence between fractions and decimal notation	79	41–43
Money and financial mathematics			
Solve problems involving purchases and the calculation of change to the nearest five cents with and without digital technologies	★ Recognise that not all countries use dollars and cents	80	44

© Australian Curriculum, Assessment and Reporting Authority 2010.

NUMBER and ALGEBRA (continued)	ELABORATIONS	ACMNA	PAGE
Patterns and algebra			
Explore and describe number patterns resulting from performing multiplication	★ Identify everyday life number patterns	81	52
Solve word problems by using number sentences involving multiplication or division where there is no remainder	★ Represent word problems as a number sentence ★ Write a word problem to match a number sentence	82	49–51
Use equivalent number sentences involving addition and subtraction to find unknown quantities	★ Write number sentences to represent and answer questions ★ Use partitioning to find unknown quantities in number sentences	83	50

MEASUREMENT and GEOMETRY		ACMMG	
Units of measurement			
Use scaled instruments to measure and compare lengths, masses, capacities and temperatures	★ Read and interpret graduated scales to the nearest graduation	84	56, 60, 71–72, 77
Compare objects using familiar metric units of area and volume	★ Compare areas using grid paper ★ Compare volumes using centicubes	90	63–67 78–80
Convert between units of time	★ Identify and use the correct operation for converting units of time	85	82–84
Use am and pm notation and solve simple time problems	★ Calculate arrival and departure times, and the time required to travel between two locations	86	82, 90–92
Shape			
Compare the areas of regular and irregular shapes by informal means	★ Compare areas using metric units such as square centimetres	87	62–67
Compare and describe two dimensional shapes that result from combining and splitting common shapes, with and without the use of digital technologies	★ Identify common 2D shapes that are part of composite shapes ★ Create 2D shapes from verbal or written instructions	88	66–67 115–122
Location and transformation			
Use simple scales, legends and directions to interpret information contained in basic maps	★ Identify the scale used on different maps and describe the differences ★ Use directions to find features on a map	90	140 141–144
Create symmetrical patterns, pictures and shapes with and without digital technologies	★ Use stimulus material such as textiles and artefacts around the world	91	123–125
Geometric reasoning			
Compare angles and classify them as equal to, greater than or less than a right angle	★ Create angles and compare them to a right angle	89	129–136

© Australian Curriculum, Assessment and Reporting Authority 2010.

STATISTICS and PROBABILITY		ACMSP	
Chance			
Describe possible everyday events and order their chances of occurring	★ List familiar events and order them from 'least likely' to 'most likely'	92	146–150
Identify events where the chance of one will not be affected by the occurrence of the other	★ Explain why a new baby can be either a girl or a boy	94	149
Data representation and interpretation			
Select and trial methods for data collection, including survey questions and recording sheets	★ Compare effectiveness of different collection methods ★ Choose the most effective way to collect data for a given investigation	95	151–152
Construct suitable data displays, with and without the use of digital technologies, from given or collected data. Include tables, column graphs and picture graphs where one picture can represent many data values	★ Explore different ways to present data	96	153–159

© Australian Curriculum, Assessment and Reporting Authority 2010.

HOW TO USE THIS BOOK

Mathematics is a way of thinking. It helps you understand how the world works. *Blake's Maths Guide for Years 3 and 4* helps you see mathematics all around you. This Guide helps you to talk about, to draw and to record mathematics. You will have the tools that you need to be a successful mathematician.

The definitions are clear, concise and written in friendly language. Real-life photographs show you what mathematics is being discussed and how it is used.

In the TRY THIS sections, you practise, make or imagine mathematical concepts. This helps you put the maths ideas inside your head. Selected answers are at the back of the book.

Blake's Maths Guide for Years 3 and 4 contains an index for locating the specific mathematical concept that you might need more information about. A glossary is also provided for quick reference.

This Guide is a vital reference for anyone wanting to be successful at years 3 and 4 mathematics.

ABOUT THE AUTHOR

Bev Dunbar is a highly respected mathematics educator. Over the last 35 years, Bev has worked extensively with students, student teachers, parents and teachers within both government and non-government education systems. She has also lectured in Mathematics Education at the University of Sydney and the Australian Catholic University. Bev is the author of many educational resources, including *Times Tables 1* and *2*, 16 books for teachers in *The Exploring Maths* series and 10 books for students in the *Excel Maths Early Skill* series.

Bev is dedicated to helping you understand and enjoy Mathematics. Her personal interests include a passion for painting and recreating medieval artworks and, of course, unravelling challenging sudokus.

PLACE VALUE TO 10 000

EVEN NUMBERS

Lots of things come in pairs. For example, eyes, arms, legs, ears and wings. You can skip count by 2s to find out how many things altogether.

2   4   6   8   10   12   14   16

Even numbers can be put into pairs, or groups of 2. When placed into pairs, there is nothing left over.

The 14 counters are placed in groups of 2, with no counters left over.

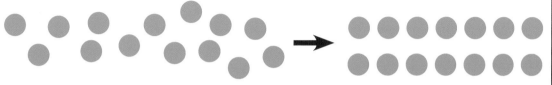

There is an easy way to work out if a number is even. Look at the last digit, the ones digit on the right. If the digit is 0, 2, 4, 6 or 8, then the whole number is **even**.

376 ones digit is a **6**, so 376 is even

It does not matter if every other digit is odd, the whole number will still be even.

77 538 ones digit is an **8**, so 77 538 is even

This means that you do not have to put everything into pairs first.

Even numbers are always divisible by 2. They are multiples of 2. The ones digit is always 0, 2, 4, 6 or 8.

Try this

1 Circle the even numbers: **33, 69, 42, 58**
2 Circle the even numbers: **104, 235, 476, 702**
3 Circle the even numbers: **1098, 3974, 4621, 7030**

ODD NUMBERS

When you put an **odd number** into pairs, there will always be one left over.

There is an easy way to work out if a number is odd. Look at the last digit, the ones digit on the right. If this digit is a 1, 3, 5, 7 or 9, then the whole number is **odd**.

479 ones digit is a 9, so 479 is odd

It does not matter if every other digit is even, the whole number will still be odd.

40263 ones digit is a 3, so 40263 is odd

Any number that ends in a 1, 3, 5, 7 or 9 is odd.

Try this

1 Circle the odd numbers: **51, 77, 82, 93**

2 Circle the odd numbers: **206, 436, 695, 849**

3 Circle the odd numbers: **3999, 5002, 7354, 8833**

A funny thing happens though. If you add 2 even numbers, the total is still even. But, if you add 2 odd numbers, the total is always even. The extra ones in each number join up to make a new pair.

13 + 7 = 20 ones digit is a 0, so 20 is even

NUMBERS TO 10000

Long ago, people worked out an easy way to count. They put things in groups of 10. People think we got the idea because we have 10 fingers and 10 toes.

This counting system is called **base 10**.

It uses only the **digits**:

0, 1, 2, 3, 4, 5, 6, 7, 8 and 9

You make numbers of any size from one digit to infinity using a **place value** system of 1s, 10s, 100s, 1000s and more.

TENS AND ONES

Numbers from 10 to 99 are all two-digit numbers. Whole numbers smaller than 10 and any leftover numbers from counting out a group of 10 are called **ones**. Numbers from 0 to 9 are one-digit numbers.

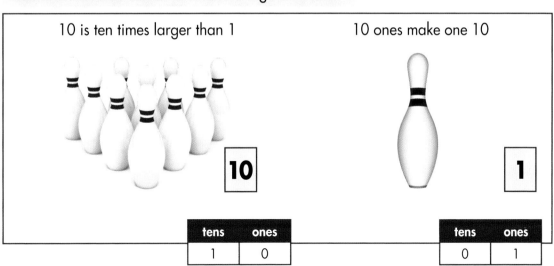

10 is ten times larger than 1   10 ones make one 10

tens	ones
1	0

tens	ones
0	1

You can count tens from 10 to 90.

10 20 30 40 50 60 70 80 90

You can **model 10s and 1s.**

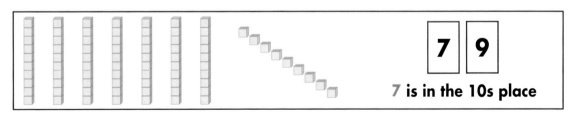

7 9

7 is in the 10s place

Try this

TENS AND ONES (continued)

You can **draw 10s and 1s** as jumps along a number line. This number line shows **48**.

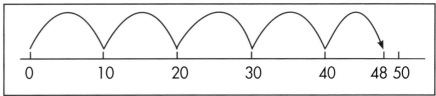

You can **say 10s and 1s** using different number names.

54 ones is the same as **5 tens and 4 ones**

How many paperclips?

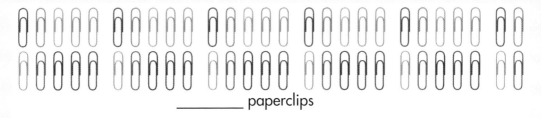

_____ paperclips

HUNDREDS

Numbers from 100 to 999 are all three-digit numbers. When you collect ten groups of 10, you regroup them as a new unit called **hundreds**.

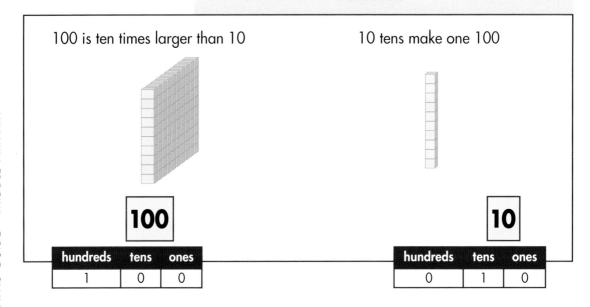

100 is ten times larger than 10

10 tens make one 100

100

hundreds	tens	ones
1	0	0

10

hundreds	tens	ones
0	1	0

You can count hundreds from 100 to 900.

100   200   300   400   500   600   700   800   900

You can **model 100s, 10s and 1s**.

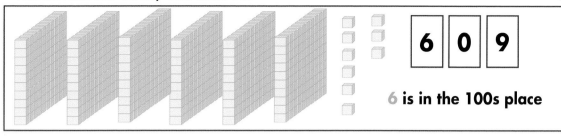

6 is in the 100s place

You can **draw 100s, 10s and 1s** as jumps along a number line.

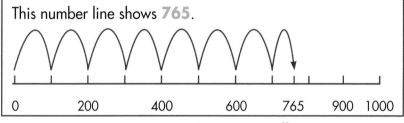

This number line shows **765**.

The world's second largest meteorite crater is at Wolfe Creek WA. It has a diameter of about 875 m.

You can **say 100s, 10s and 1s** using different number names.

hundreds	tens	ones	number names
8	7	5	8 hundreds, 7 tens, 5 ones
8	7	5	87 tens, 5 ones
8	7	5	875 ones

In words this is 'eight hundred and seventy-five'.

Ordering three-digit numbers

You can use rules to rearrange and make different three-digit numbers.

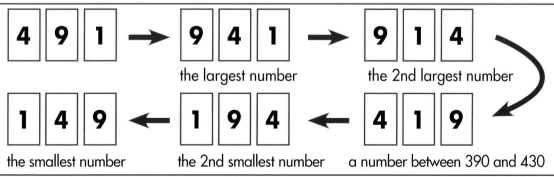

the largest number

the 2nd largest number

the smallest number

the 2nd smallest number

a number between 390 and 430

How can we rearrange these three cards to make:

1 the number closest to 500?

2 the smallest number?

3 a number between 550 and 600?

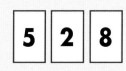

Try this

THOUSANDS

Numbers from 1000 to 9999 are all four-digit numbers. When you collect ten groups of 100, you regroup them as a new unit called **thousands**.

1000 is ten times larger than 100

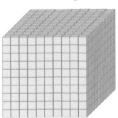

1000

thousands	hundreds	tens	ones
Th	H	T	O
1000s	100s	10s	1s
1	0	0	0

10 hundreds make one 1000

100

thousands	hundreds	tens	ones
Th	H	T	O
1000s	100s	10s	1s
0	1	0	0

Australian money does not have a $1000 note.

You can count thousands from 1000 to 9000.

1000 2000 3000 4000 5000 6000 7000 8000 9000

There are special words for some groups of 1000.

1000 m = 1 km

1000 mL = 1 L

1000 kg = 1 tonne

You can **model 1000s, 100s, 10s and 1s.**

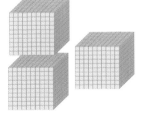

| 3 | 2 | 7 | 0 |

3 is in the 1000s place

You can **draw 1000s, 100s, 10s and 1s** as jumps along a number line. This number line shows **5627**.

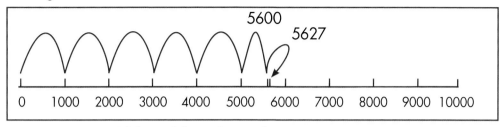

You can **say 1000s, 100s, 10s and 1s** using different number names.

1000s	100s	10s	1s	number names
9	0	5	4	9 thousands, 0 hundreds, 5 tens and 4 ones
9	0	5	4	90 hundreds, 5 tens and 4 ones
9	0	5	4	905 tens and 4 ones
9	0	5	4	9054 ones

In words this is '**nine thousand and fifty-four**'.

Ordering four-digit numbers

Remember that 1000s are ten times larger than 100s. So 1001 is larger than 999, even though it has two 1s and two 0s in it. It is not the digit but the position of a digit that matters.

You can use ordering rules to rearrange and make different four-digit numbers.

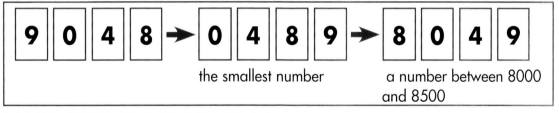

the smallest number   a number between 8000 and 8500

Match these numbers to their labels:

1 the number closest to 3500

2 the largest number

3 a number between 4500 and 5000

4 a number with 9 in the 10s place

Try this

Mount Everest is 8850 metres high. It is the tallest mountain in the world.

You can leave a space before the hundreds digit so it is easier to read. Which is easier to read? 43 987 or 43987

TEN THOUSAND

Numbers from 10 000 to 99 999 are all five-digit numbers. When you collect ten groups of 1000, you regroup them as a new unit called **tens of thousands**.

10000 is ten times larger than 1000
10 thousands make one 10 000

Large numbers are hard to model with blocks. Use coloured counters instead.

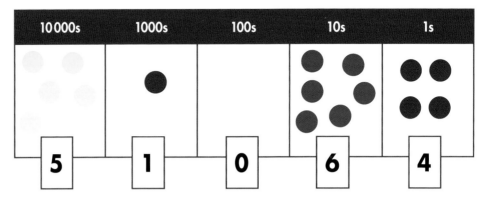

10 000s	1000s	100s	10s	1s
5	1	0	6	4

5 is in the 10 000s place

In words this is 'fifty-one thousand, and sixty-four'.

Challenge

If your mum earns $51 064 in a year, how much is that a week?

You can use a calculator here.

$_____ in a week

Ordering five-digit numbers

You can put a mixture of large numbers in order by looking at the digits.

The number with the most digits is the largest.

$45 231

$9878

$45 231 is more than $9878 because $45 231 has 5 digits. $9878 has only 4 digits.

Circle the larger number.

1 712 L OR 1001 L

2 $5999 OR $899

3 5893 kg OR 17055 kg

4 10401 m OR 8652 m

Try this

If you have the same number of digits, look at the left digit first.

The larger number has the larger digit on the left.

> An elephant has a mass of about 5004 kg.
> A rhinoceros has a mass of about 2999 kg.
> 5004 kg is larger than 2999 kg because there is a 5 in the thousands place. 2999 only has a 2 in the thousands place.

Circle the larger number.

1 $6050 OR $8712

2 23495 m OR 37055 m

Try this

PLACE VALUE NAMES

When you put the digits 0 – 9 together to make a number, the digits are in a specific order that matters. They have **place value**.

$8300 is more than $3800

The 8 in $8300 is ten times larger than the 8 in $3800.

The Andes in South America is the longest mountain range in the world. It is 7242 km long. This is a fact. You cannot rearrange these digits to make a new number like 4227 km, and then say that this is the length of the Andes. Each digit has a special meaning.

Each digit in a number has a place value that you write in columns like this number:

TT Th H T O
7 8 2 3 9

7 is in the **ten thousands place**
8 is in the **thousands place**
2 is in the **hundreds place**
3 is in the **tens place**
9 is in the **ones place**

Try this

Circle the larger value of 5 in each pair of numbers.

1 56000 or 35999

2 8957 or 1500

3 572 or 9005

4 15366 or 23566

ADDITION & SUBTRACTION

You use different words to talk about **addition**:

add   total   and   plus   more than   combine   join

+	add
=	is exactly the same number as
sum	the total or answer to an addition problem

7 + 8 = 15

You use different words to talk about **subtraction**:

take away   subtract   minus   remove   less than

-	subtract
=	is exactly the same number as
difference	the answer to a subtraction problem

7 = 15 − 8

ADDING & SUBTRACTING FACT FAMILY

Addition and subtraction are linked together in fact families.

Once you know one fact, you really know four facts.

Think addition when doing subtraction.

14 − 8 = ☐ is the same as saying

8 + ☐ = 14

8 + 6 = 14
14 − 6 = 8
6 + 8 = 14
14 − 8 = 6

But you can also write them this way:

14 = 8 + 6
8 = 14 − 6
14 = 6 + 8
6 = 14 − 8

So there are 8 different ways to record every fact.

Think of the Fact Family Triangle each time you remember a fact.

Once you know all your quick recall facts for addition and subtraction, you can use these facts to solve problems mentally. This is without using your fingers or pencil and paper calculations.

Try this

Try to finish each set in less than 1 minute with no mistakes.

Set 1

8 + 7		3 + 5		9 + 10		7 + 7		5 + 4	
2 + 9		4 + 3		0 + 8		1 + 7		6 + 5	

Set 2

15 – 6		19 – 9		17 – 9		10 – 6		13 – 8	
14 – 9		9 – 3		11 – 7		12 – 9		16 – 10	

Challenge

1 If 7 + 6 = 13, what is 307 + 6? Why?
what is 2007 + 6? Why?

2 If 16 – 9 = 7, what is 516 – 9? Why?
what is 3016 – 9? Why?

FACTS TO 20

You are a Maths Star when you know all your basic facts.

Practise until you remember each answer without making a mistake.

+/–	0	1	2	3	4	5	6	7	8	9	10
0	0	1	2	3	4	5	6	7	8	9	10
1	1	2	3	4	5	6	7	8	9	10	11
2	2	3	4	5	6	7	8	9	10	11	12
3	3	4	5	6	7	8	9	10	11	12	13
4	4	5	6	7	8	9	10	11	12	13	14
5	5	6	7	8	9	10	11	12	13	14	15
6	6	7	8	9	10	11	12	13	14	15	16
7	7	8	9	10	11	12	13	14	15	16	17
8	8	9	10	11	12	13	14	15	16	17	18
9	9	10	11	12	13	14	15	16	17	18	19
10	10	11	12	13	14	15	16	17	18	19	20

To find an addition fact: read down a column and across a row to find where they join.

To find a subtraction fact: start from a middle number and read back to the start of a row and up to the start of a column.

1 How many different patterns can you spot in the table?

2 What do you see if you read:

a across a row? **b** down a column? **c** along a diagonal?

Try this

MENTAL STRATEGIES FOR ADDING & SUBTRACTING

Doubles

double   2 times   2 ×
twice as many
2 groups of

Whole number doubles are always even numbers.

Double	0	1	2	3	4	5	6	7	8	9	10
	0	2	4	6	8	10	12	14	16	18	20

Double	10	11	12	13	14	15	16	17	18	19	20
	20	22	24	26	28	30	32	34	36	38	40

You can extend the 0 – 10 facts when you multiply by 10.

Double	0	10	20	30	40	50	60	70	80	90	100
	0	20	40	60	80	100	120	140	160	180	200

You can extend the 0 – 10 facts when you multiply by 100.

Double	0	100	200	300	400	500	600	700	800	900	1000
	0	200	400	600	800	1000	1200	1400	1600	1800	2000

Halves

half of   halve
put into 2 equal groups $\frac{1}{2}$ ×

When you chop something in half, the two parts are the same size.
Which two numbers add together to make the whole?

Half of	0	1	2	3	4	5	6	7	8	9	10
	0	$\frac{1}{2}$	1	$1\frac{1}{2}$	2	$2\frac{1}{2}$	3	$3\frac{1}{2}$	4	$4\frac{1}{2}$	5

Half of	10	11	12	13	14	15	16	17	18	19	20
	5	$5\frac{1}{2}$	6	$6\frac{1}{2}$	7	$7\frac{1}{2}$	8	$8\frac{1}{2}$	9	$9\frac{1}{2}$	10

You can extend the 0 – 10 facts when you multiply by 10.

Half of	0	10	20	30	40	50	60	70	80	90	100
	0	5	10	15	20	25	30	35	40	45	50

You can extend the 0 – 10 facts when you multiply by 100.

Half of	0	100	200	300	400	500	600	700	800	900	1000
	0	50	100	150	200	250	300	350	400	450	500

Adding & subtracting multiples of 10

To add multiples of 10 in your head just add the 10s digits. Remember your answer is a multiple of 10.

40 + 30   because 4 + 3 = 7, 40 + 30 = 70

90 + 30   because 9 + 3 = 12, 90 + 30 = 120

Try this

Try to finish the set in less than 1 minute with no mistakes.

50 + 20		10 + 70		60 + 40		30 + 90		80 + 20	
100 + 90		40 + 80		70 + 80		80 + 30		90 + 50	

To subtract multiples of 10 in your head, take away the 10s digits. Remember your answer is a multiple of 10.

80 – 30   because 8 – 3 = 5, 80 – 30 = 50

170 – 90 because 17 – 9 = 8, 170 – 90 = 80

Try this

Try to finish the set in less than 1 minute with no mistakes.

90 – 40		50 – 30		80 – 20		70 – 40		60 – 30	
110 – 80		130 – 70		140 – 70		180 – 90		150 – 80	

Add to make the next 10

To build any two-digit number to the next 10, just think of your quick recall facts to 10. What do you need to add?

23 + □ = 30   because 3 and 7 more make 10, 23 and 7 more make 30

82 + □ = 90   because 2 + 8 = 10, 82 and 8 more make 90

Try this

Try to finish the set in less than 1 minute with no mistakes.

25 + □ = 30		48 + □ = 50		14 + □ = 20		31 + □ = 40	
57 + □ = 60		71 + □ = 80		93 + □ = 100		86 + □ = 90	

Challenge

If 56 + 4 = 60, what is 856 + 4? Why?

MENTAL STRATEGIES FOR ADDING & SUBTRACTING (continued)

Adding a multiple of 10 to any two-digit number

Add the tens together first. Remember to then add the ones.

63 + 50

Try this

$$60 + 50 = 110$$
$$110 + 3 = 113$$

Try to finish the set in less than 1 minute with no mistakes.

23 + 50		48 + 20		39 + 60		55 + 30		65 + 20	
84 + 90		48 + 90		62 + 70		88 + 40		75 + 70	

Challenge
If 73 + 50 = 123, what is 473 + 50? Why?

Subtracting a multiple of 10 from any two-digit number

Try taking away the tens first. Remember to then add the ones.

84 – 30

Try this

$$80 - 30 = 50$$
$$50 + 4 = 54$$

Try to finish the set in less than 1 minute with no mistakes.

88 – 30		47 – 20		72 – 40		61 – 50		94 – 30	
165 – 80		147 – 70		156 – 70		138 – 90		179 – 80	

Challenge
If 96 – 40 = 56, what is 796 – 40? Why?

Adding pairs to 100

A useful mental strategy is to find number pairs that add to 100.

This skill will help you later to add large numbers in your head.

First add to the next 10. Then work out which multiple of 10 you need to make 100.

I cost $56.

How much change from $100?

$56 + $4 = $60

$60 + $40 = $100

You will get $44 change from $100

I am 68 cm high. How much do I need to grow before I am 100 cm?

68 cm + 2 cm = 70 cm

70 cm + 30 cm = 100 cm

You need to grow 32 cm more

Try this

Calculate how many more make 100

1 42 cm How many more centimetres to make 100 cm?

2 53 mL How many more millilitres to make 100 mL?

3 71 g   How many more grams to make 100 g?

4 88 m² How many more square metres to make 100 m²?

ADDING ANY TWO-DIGIT NUMBERS

You can use your quick recall facts to 20 and each of the strategies to work out addition problems to 100 or more in your head.

To calculate mentally use one of the following strategies.

Try this

Add the tens first, and then add the ones.	$40 + $30 = $70 $8 + $7 = $15 $70 + $15 = $85
Add the extra ones to the first number, and then add the extra tens.	$48 + $7 = $55 $55 + $30 = $85
Add to the next ten, and then add the extras.	$48 + $2 = $50 $50 + $35 = $85
Take the second number up to the next ten, add, and then take away the difference you added.	$48 + $40 = $88 $88 – $3 = $85

Find the total to each problem mentally. Which strategy did you use?

1 $25 + $63   **2** $39 + $64   **3** $72 + $37   **4** $96 + $84

DOUBLING ANY TWO-DIGIT NUMBERS

Try this

To double any two-digit number mentally: double the 10s digit first, and then double the ones digit. Add these answers to get your total.

Double 47	2 × 86
2 × 40 = **80**	2 × 80 = **160**
2 × 7 = **14**	2 × 6 = **12**
80 + 14 = 94	160 + 12 = 172

Find the total to each problem mentally. Which strategy did you use?

1 Double 35   **2** 2 × 72   **3** Twice 86   **4** 2 groups of 94

Challenge

If double 51 is 102, what is double 510? Why?

DIFFERENT NUMBER NAMES

You can talk about a number in many different ways using addition and subtraction. You can be as creative as you like.

To measure exactly 60 grams of flour for a recipe, you can try:

$$100 \text{ g} - 40 \text{ g} = 60 \text{ g}$$
$$9 \text{ g} + 51 \text{ g} = 60 \text{ g}$$
$$79 \text{ g} - 19 \text{ g} = 60 \text{ g}$$
$$33 \text{ g} + 27 \text{ g} = 60 \text{ g}$$

And there are many more like these examples.

Challenge
Find five different ways using + and – to measure exactly 150 mL of water.

One way to create + patterns is to write numbers in a line.
Join them up like a rainbow. Then magically they all have the same total.

12 13 14 15 16 17 18 19 20

$$12 + 20 = 32$$
$$13 + 19 = 32$$
$$14 + 18 = 32$$
$$15 + 17 = 32$$
$$16 + 16 = 32$$

HALVING ANY TWO-DIGIT NUMBER

Halving is an effective mental strategy that uses your known facts for doubling.

Halving even numbers is easy. Think of your doubles.

$\frac{1}{2} \times 64$ $2 \times 32 = 64$, so half of 64 is 32

Halving odd numbers is trickier. One strategy is to break a large number up into parts that you know well.

$\frac{1}{2} \times 95$ 95 is the same as 90 + 5,
so halve each part
Half of 90 is 45
Half of 5 is $2\frac{1}{2}$
So, half of 95 is $45 + 2\frac{1}{2} = 47\frac{1}{2}$

Try this

1 Half of 29

2 Put 73 into 2 equal groups

3 $\frac{1}{2} \times 88$

4 Halve 99

Challenge
If half of 82 is 41, what is half of 820? Why?

MULTIPLICATION & DIVISION

MULTIPLICATION

Multiplication is a fast way to add. It saves you having to add up all the numbers one by one. It only works when you are adding the same number each time. It is repeated addition.

Jack has a caterpillar.

It has 9 pairs of legs.

How many legs altogether?

2 + 2 + 2 + 2 + 2 + 2 + 2 + 2 + 2

This is the same as 9 × 2 =18 legs

Here are a few ways to talk about multiplication.

the product of

groups of   **piles of**

multiplied by

times

rows of

Arrays

An **array** is a set of objects in rows and columns.

If you read the rows, this is **3 × 4**.

If you read the columns, this is **4 × 3**.

Both have the same number of objects.

3 × 4 array

Multiples

When you **skip count** by the same number you get multiples.

0   7   14   21   28   35   42   49

These are all multiples of **7**.

Patterns

You can **look for patterns** in the multiples.

Look at the last digit, the ones digit.

The last digit pattern for **6** is

0 6 12 18 24 30 36 42 48 54 60

So, if a number ends in a 3 it is not a multiple of 6.

Add the digits

If you add the digits in each multiple, you make another pattern.

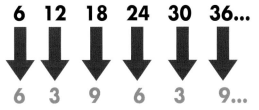

6   12   18   24   30   36...

6   3   9   6   3   9...

Multiplication facts

The symbol for multiplication is **✗**.

6 ✗ 4 = 24

The answer to a multiplication problem is called a **product**.

The **product of 3 and 5** is **15** or 3 × 5 = 15

Your basic facts are called multiplication tables because you usually see them in a grid or table.

You will be brilliant at multiplication if you remember all your facts. Start with quick recall for 2s to 20, 5s to 50 and 10s to 100.

GROUPS OF 2

Some things come in **pairs**.

Pair of shoes   Pair of ears

You can make a **2s array**.

Can you say these numbers quickly and in order, with your eyes shut?

**0   2   4   6   8   10   12
14   16   18   20**

These are all **multiples of 2**.

You can **skip count by 2** to find out how many altogether.

… 66, 68, 70, 72 … 196, 198, 200, 202 … 694, 696, 698, 700 …

You can use a **multiplication pattern** to show all the multiples of 2 to 100. The 'last digit' pattern for multiples of 2 is

0, 2, 4, 6, 8, 0, 2, 4, 6, 8...

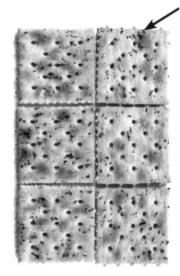

2 × 3 array

1	2	3	4	5	6	7	8	9	10
11	12	13	14	15	16	17	18	19	20
21	22	23	24	25	26	27	28	29	30
31	32	33	34	35	36	37	38	39	40
41	42	43	44	45	46	47	48	49	50
51	52	53	54	55	56	57	58	59	60
61	62	63	64	65	66	67	68	69	70
71	72	73	74	75	76	77	78	79	80
81	82	83	84	85	86	87	88	89	90
91	92	93	94	95	96	97	98	99	100

You can **teach your calculator to multiply by 2** using repeated addition. Press

You can **solve problems about groups of 2**.

How much for 6 bunches?

$2 + $2 + $2 + $2 + $2 + $2

6 × $2 = $12

How much change from $20?

20 − 12 = 8

So you get $8 change

0 × 2 = 0	6 × 2 = 12
1 × 2 = 2	7 × 2 = 14
2 × 2 = 4	8 × 2 = 16
3 × 2 = 6	9 × 2 = 18
4 × 2 = 8	10 × 2 = 20
5 × 2 = 10	

You are a Maths Star if you can **recall all these facts for 2** without making a mistake.

Try this

Solve these number problems

1 How many feet on 9 T-rex toys? _____ feet

2 How many eyes on 10 people? _____ eyes

3 How many legs on 7 chickens? _____ legs

4 How many litres do you have in eight 2 L bottles of drink?

_____ litres of drink

Challenge

Your sister puts $2 a day in her money box. How much will she save in 4 weeks?

She will save $_____

GROUPS OF 5

Some things come in **5s**.

5 arms

5 sides

You can make a **5s array**.

5 × 4 array

Can you say these numbers quickly and in order, with your eyes shut?

**0   5   10   15   20   25   30
35   40   45   50**

These are all **multiples of 5**.

You can **skip count by 5** to find out how many altogether.

… 65, 70, 75, 80 … 195, 200, 205, 210 … 695, 700, 705 …

You can use a **multiplication pattern** to show all the multiples of 5 to 100. The 'last digit' pattern for multiples of 5 is

0, 5, 0, 5...

1	2	3	4	5	6	7	8	9	10
11	12	13	14	15	16	17	18	19	20
21	22	23	24	25	26	27	28	29	30
31	32	33	34	35	36	37	38	39	40
41	42	43	44	45	46	47	48	49	50
51	52	53	54	55	56	57	58	59	60
61	62	63	64	65	66	67	68	69	70
71	72	73	74	75	76	77	78	79	80
81	82	83	84	85	86	87	88	89	90
91	92	93	94	95	96	97	98	99	100

You can **teach your calculator to multiply by 5** using repeated addition. Press

You can **solve problems about groups of 5**.

How much for 10 robots?

5 + 5 + 5 + 5 + 5 + 5 + 5 + 5 + 5 + 5

10 × $5 = $50

How much change from $100?

100 − 50 = 50

So you get $50 change

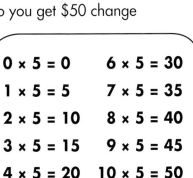

0 × 5 = 0	6 × 5 = 30
1 × 5 = 5	7 × 5 = 35
2 × 5 = 10	8 × 5 = 40
3 × 5 = 15	9 × 5 = 45
4 × 5 = 20	10 × 5 = 50
5 × 5 = 25	

You are a Maths Star if you **recall all these facts for 5** without making a mistake.

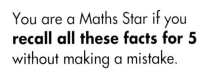

Try this

Solve these number problems

1 Six people win a lottery and get $5 each. How much do they win altogether? $_____

2 How many sides on 5 pentagons? _____ sides

3 How many fingers and toes altogether on 6 hands and 4 feet? _____ fingers and toes

4 How many metres altogether if you have six 5 m ropes?

_____ metres of rope

Challenge

A cube has 5 dots on each face. How many dots on 3 cubes like the one shown? _____ dots

GROUPS OF 10

Some things come in **10s**.

10 toes $10 notes

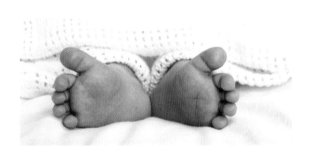

You can make a **10s array**.

Can you say these numbers quickly and in order, with your eyes shut?

0   10   20   30   40   50   60   70   80   90   100

These are all **multiples of 10**

You can **skip count by 10** to find out how many altogether.

40, 50, 60 … 190, 200, 210 … 880, 890, 900 …

You can use a **multiplication pattern** to show all the multiples of 10 to 100. The 'last digit' pattern for multiples of 10 is

0, 0, 0...

1	2	3	4	5	6	7	8	9	10
11	12	13	14	15	16	17	18	19	20
21	22	23	24	25	26	27	28	29	30
31	32	33	34	35	36	37	38	39	40
41	42	43	44	45	46	47	48	49	50
51	52	53	54	55	56	57	58	59	60
61	62	63	64	65	66	67	68	69	70
71	72	73	74	75	76	77	78	79	80
81	82	83	84	85	86	87	88	89	90
91	92	93	94	95	96	97	98	99	100

You can **teach your calculator to multiply by 10** using repeated addition. Press

You can **solve problems about groups of 10**.

How much for 9 toy dogs?

$10 + 10 + 10 + 10 + 10 + 10 + 10 + 10 + 10$

$9 \times \$10 = \$90$

How much change from $100?

$100 - 90 = 10$

So you get $10 change

$0 \times 10 = 0$	$6 \times 10 = 60$
$1 \times 10 = 10$	$7 \times 10 = 70$
$2 \times 10 = 20$	$8 \times 10 = 80$
$3 \times 10 = 30$	$9 \times 10 = 90$
$4 \times 10 = 40$	$10 \times 10 = 100$
$5 \times 10 = 50$	

You are a Maths Star if you **recall all these facts for 10** without making a mistake.

Try this

Solve these number problems

1 How much for 8 hamburgers at $10 each?

$ _____

2 How many sides on 4 decagons?

_____ sides

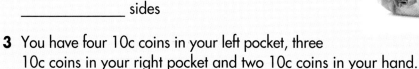

3 You have four 10c coins in your left pocket, three 10c coins in your right pocket and two 10c coins in your hand.

How much altogether? _____ cents

Challenge

How many fingers and toes altogether in a group of 9 people?

_____ fingers and toes

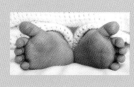 

DIVISION

Division is a fast way to subtract. It only works when you are taking away the same number each time. It is repeated subtraction.

Division is the opposite of multiplication. When you remember all your multiplication facts, you will also know all your division facts.

5 L

Jess pours 40 litres of water equally into some five-litre containers.

How many 5 L containers does she need?

40 – 5 – 5 – 5 – 5 – 5 – 5 – 5 – 5

40 put into groups of 5 is 8

40 ÷ 5 = 8

So Jess needs 8 five-litre containers.

Here are a few ways to talk about division.

shared between

put into groups of

divided by

put into rows of

shared among

Factors

Factors are the two whole numbers you multiply to get a product.

12 ÷ 2 = 6 or **6 × 2 = 12**

So 2 and 6 are both factors of 12

Division facts

The symbol for division is ÷.

27 ÷ 3 = 9

The answer to a division problem is a **quotient**.

35 divided into 7 equal parts makes a quotient of 5.

35 ÷ 7 = 5

You will be brilliant at division if you remember all your facts.

Start with quick recall for 2s from 20, 5s from 50 and 10s from 100.

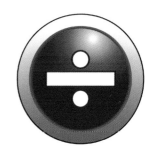

MULTIPLYING & DIVIDING FACT FAMILY

Most people find it easier to do division by thinking multiplication.

70 ÷ 10 is the same as 10 × □ = 70

Remember your family of facts.

If you know that 8 × 5 = 40, you also know

5 × 8 = 40

40 ÷ 8 = 5

40 ÷ 5 = 8

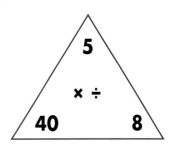

Remember you can write these like this too.

40 = 8 × 5	5 = 40 ÷ 8
40 = 5 × 8	8 = 40 ÷ 5

So there are 8 different ways to record every fact.

Think of the Fact Family Triangle each time you remember a fact.

GROUPS OF 3

Many things are **counted in 3s**.

3 wheels

3 sides

These numbers are all **multiples of 3**.

3 × 4 array

0 3 6 9 12 15 18 21 24 27 30

You can make a **3s array**.

Digit patterns of 3

Multiples	3	6	9	12	15	18	21	24	27
Add digits	3	6	9	1 + 2	1 + 5	1+ 8	2 + 1	2 + 4	2 + 7
Total	3	6	9	3	6	9	3	6	9

So if the digits add to 3, 6 or 9 you can tell quickly that a large number is a multiple of 3.

876,   8 + 7 + 6 = 21,   2 + 1 = 3

You can **solve problems about groups of 3**.

If 7 people at your barbeque will get 3 sausages each, how many sausages do you need to buy?

3 + 3 + 3 + 3 + 3 + 3 + 3

7 × 3 = 21

How many will be left if 3 people do not come?

3 × 3 = 9 so you will have 9 sausages left over.

0 × 3 = 0	6 × 3 = 18
1 × 3 = 3	7 × 3 = 21
2 × 3 = 6	8 × 3 = 24
3 × 3 = 9	9 × 3 = 27
4 × 3 = 12	10 × 3 = 30
5 × 3 = 15	

You are a Maths Star if you **recall all these facts for 3** without making a mistake.

GROUPS OF 4

Many things are counted in 4s.

4 wheels

4 sides

These numbers are all **multiples of 4**.

0 4 8 12 16 20 24 28 32 36 40

You can make a **4s array**.

4 × 6 array

You can **solve problems about groups of 4**.

There are 4 horses in each paddock. How many horses in 9 paddocks?

4 + 4 + 4 + 4 + 4 + 4 + 4 + 4 + 4

$9 \times 4 = 36$

How many horses if there is one more paddock?

$36 + 4 = 40$

So there will be 40 horses

You are a Maths Star if you **recall all these facts for 4** without making a mistake.

$0 \times 4 = 0$	$6 \times 4 = 24$
$1 \times 4 = 4$	$7 \times 4 = 28$
$2 \times 4 = 8$	$8 \times 4 = 32$
$3 \times 4 = 12$	$9 \times 4 = 36$
$4 \times 4 = 16$	$10 \times 4 = 40$
$5 \times 4 = 20$	

GROUPS OF 6

Many things are **counted in 6s**.

6 legs

6 sides

These numbers are all **multiples of 6**.

0 6 12 18 24 30 36 42 48 54 60

You can make a **6s array**.

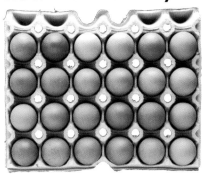

6 × 4 array

You can **solve problems about groups of 6**.

How much change from $50 if you buy 6 toy ducks?

6 + 6 + 6 + 6 + 6 + 6

6 × 6 = 36

36 + 14 = 50

So you will get $14 change

$6

0 × 6 = 0	6 × 6 = 36
1 × 6 = 6	7 × 6 = 42
2 × 6 = 12	8 × 6 = 48
3 × 6 = 18	9 × 6 = 54
4 × 6 = 24	10 × 6 = 60
5 × 6 = 30	

You are a Maths Star if you **recall all these facts for 6** without making a mistake.

GROUPS OF 7

Many things are counted in **7s**.

7 days in a week

7 sides

These numbers are all **multiples of 7**.

0   7   14   21   28   35   42   49   56   63   70

You can make a **7s array**.

7 × 6 array

You can **solve problems about groups of 7**.

I saved $7 a week for 8 weeks.

$7 + 7 + 7 + 7 + 7 + 7 + 7 + 7$

$8 × 7 = 56$

I saved $56 altogether.

You are a Maths Star if you **recall all these facts for 7** without making a mistake.

0 × 7 = 0	6 × 7 = 42
1 × 7 = 7	7 × 7 = 49
2 × 7 = 14	8 × 7 = 56
3 × 7 = 21	9 × 7 = 63
4 × 7 = 28	10 × 7 = 70
5 × 7 = 35	

GROUPS OF 8

Many things are **counted in 8s.**

8 legs   8 sides

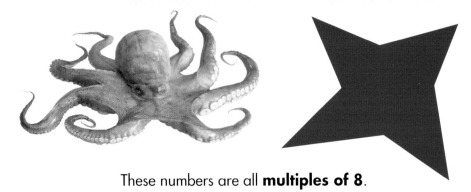

These numbers are all **multiples of 8**.

0   8   16   24   32   40   48   56   64   72   80

You can make an **8s array**.

8 × 4 array

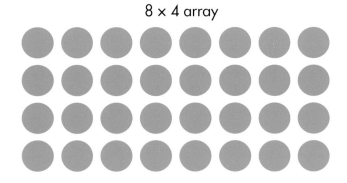

You can **solve problems about groups of 8**.

Each wall is 8 m². There are 4 walls to paint.

How much paint will I need?

8 + 8 + 8 + 8 or 4 × 8 = 32

I need to paint 32 m².

0 × 8 = 0	6 × 8 = 48
1 × 8 = 8	7 × 8 = 56
2 × 8 = 16	8 × 8 = 64
3 × 8 = 24	9 × 8 = 72
4 × 8 = 32	10 × 8 = 80
5 × 8 = 40	

You are a Maths Star if you **recall all these facts for 8** without making a mistake.

GROUPS OF 9

Many things are **counted in 9s.**

$9 a tin

9 sides

These numbers are all **multiples of 9.**

0   9   18   27   36   45   54   63   72   81   90

You can make a **9s array**.

9 × 3 array

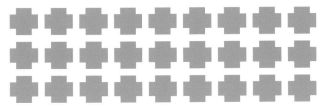

You can **solve problems about groups of 9**.

Each classroom is 9 m long. We have
6 classrooms in a line.

How long are all the classrooms together?

9 + 9 + 9 + 9 + 9 + 9

or 6 × 9 = 54

They measure 54 m altogether.

You are a Maths Star if you **recall all these facts for 9** without making a mistake.

0 × 9 = 0	6 × 9 = 54
1 × 9 = 9	7 × 9 = 63
2 × 9 = 18	8 × 9 = 72
3 × 9 = 27	9 × 9 = 81
4 × 9 = 36	10 × 9 = 90
5 × 9 = 45	

TIMES TABLES GRID

This is a summary of all your × and ÷ table facts.
You need to know them off by heart.

×/÷	0	1	2	3	4	5	6	7	8	9	10
0	0	0	0	0	0	0	0	0	0	0	0
1	0	1	2	3	4	5	6	7	8	9	10
2	0	2	4	6	8	10	12	14	16	18	20
3	0	3	6	9	12	15	18	21	24	27	30
4	0	4	8	12	16	20	24	28	32	36	40
5	0	5	10	15	20	25	30	35	40	45	50
6	0	6	12	18	24	30	36	42	48	54	60
7	0	7	14	21	28	35	42	49	56	63	70
8	0	8	16	24	32	40	48	56	64	72	80
9	0	9	18	27	36	45	54	63	72	81	90
10	0	10	20	30	40	50	60	70	80	90	100

- All the yellow facts are easy 0 ×, 1 × and 10 ×

- All the green facts are repeats. Remember your fact families. If you know 8 × 4 = 32, then you also know

  4 × 8 = 32 or 32 ÷ 4 = 8.

- All the white facts are the 36 essential facts you may not know. Focus on recalling these with perfect accuracy.

Try this

Look down each column in the grid shown above. You can see the pattern of multiples.

How many other patterns can you discover?

Challenge

You can extend your × facts by multiplying by 10 in your head.

70 × 6 = 10 × 7 × 6

7 × 6 = 42 so 70 × 6 = 10 × 42   That's 420.

Let's try another one.

90 × 3 = 10 × 9 × 3

9 × 3 = 27 so 90 × 3 = 10 × 27   That's 270.

FRACTIONS & DECIMALS

FRACTIONS

Not all numbers are whole numbers. You can divide an object into equal size parts to create fractions.

When you **cut** an object into equal size parts, you create fractions.

A block of cheese

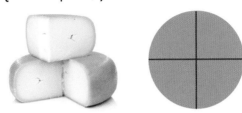

- 4 equal parts
- 4 quarters
- $4 \times \dfrac{1}{4}$

When you **fold** an object into equal size parts, you create fractions.

A paper square

- 3 equal parts
- 3 thirds

- $\dfrac{1}{3} + \dfrac{1}{3} + \dfrac{1}{3}$
- $3 \times \dfrac{1}{3}$

When you **sort** objects into smaller equal size groups, you create fractions.

A chair with 5 pups

- 5 equal parts
- 5 fifths

- $\dfrac{1}{5} + \dfrac{1}{5} + \dfrac{1}{5} + \dfrac{1}{5} + \dfrac{1}{5}$
- $5 \times \dfrac{1}{5}$

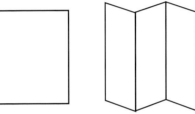

When you **divide a length** into smaller equal size lengths, you create fractions.

10 cm

- 10 equal parts
- 10 tenths

- $\dfrac{1}{10} + \dfrac{1}{10} + \dfrac{1}{10} + \dfrac{1}{10} + \dfrac{1}{10} + \dfrac{1}{10} + \dfrac{1}{10} + \dfrac{1}{10} + \dfrac{1}{10} + \dfrac{1}{10}$
- $10 \times \dfrac{1}{10}$

When you **divide a number line** into smaller equal size lengths, you create fractions.

100

- 10 equal parts
- 10 tenths
- $\dfrac{1}{10} + \dfrac{1}{10} + \dfrac{1}{10} + \dfrac{1}{10} + \dfrac{1}{10} + \dfrac{1}{10} + \dfrac{1}{10} + \dfrac{1}{10} + \dfrac{1}{10} + \dfrac{1}{10}$
- $10 \times \dfrac{1}{10}$

FRACTION LANGUAGE

The numbers and symbols in a fraction have special names

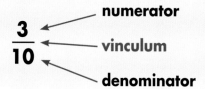

$$\frac{3}{10}$$

numerator
vinculum
denominator

$$\frac{3}{10}$$ numerator
denominator

The **denominator** is the bottom number. It tells you how many equal parts in the whole object or set of objects.

The **numerator** is the top number. It tells you how many of those equal parts you have or want.

The larger the numerator the more equal parts you are talking about.

   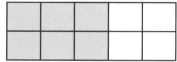

$$\frac{2}{10}$$ $$\frac{6}{10}$$

Try this

1 Draw and shade $\frac{3}{4}$

2 Draw and shade $\frac{8}{10}$

3 Show where these fractions are on the number lines:
$$\frac{2}{3} \quad \frac{3}{4} \quad \frac{6}{10} \quad \frac{2}{5}$$

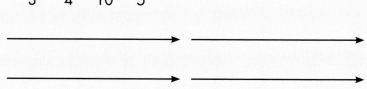

HALVES, QUARTERS & EIGHTHS

If you chop one tomato into 2 equal parts, then you get
2 **halves**.

Halves are 2 equal parts.

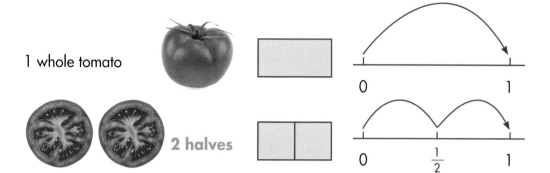

1 whole tomato

2 halves

If you chop each half into 2 equal parts, then you get
4 **quarters**.

Quarters are 4 equal parts. Each one is a half of a half.

4 quarters

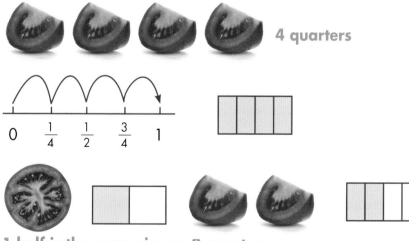

1 half is the same size as 2 quarters

4 quarters are the same size as 1 whole

HALVES, QUARTERS & EIGHTHS (continued)

4 quarters $= \dfrac{4}{4} = 1$

So, 8 quarters are the same as 2 whole tomatoes.

8 quarters = $\dfrac{8}{4}$ = 2

If you chop 4 quarters each into 2 equal parts, then you get 8 **eighths**.

Eighths are 8 equal parts.

$$\frac{4}{4} = \frac{8}{8} \qquad \frac{3}{4} = \frac{6}{8} \qquad \frac{2}{4} = \frac{4}{8} \qquad \frac{1}{4} = \frac{2}{8}$$

$$0 \qquad \frac{1}{8} \qquad \frac{2}{8} \qquad \frac{3}{8} \qquad \frac{4}{8} \qquad \frac{5}{8} \qquad \frac{6}{8} \qquad \frac{7}{8} \qquad 1$$

MORE HALVES, QUARTERS & EIGHTHS

Halves

$\dfrac{1}{2}$ of a jug of milk $\dfrac{1}{2}$ of the baubles $\dfrac{1}{2}$ past 12 o'clock

Quarters   ### Eighths

$\dfrac{1}{4}$ of a strawberry

$\dfrac{1}{8}$ of the limes

$\dfrac{1}{4}$ of the dogs

$\dfrac{1}{8}$ of an octagon

Counting by halves, quarters & eighths

If the numerator is the same number as the denominator, then you have a whole object or one whole set of objects.

This is how you count by **halves**:

$\frac{1}{2}$, 1, $1\frac{1}{2}$, 2, $2\frac{1}{2}$, 3, $3\frac{1}{2}$, 4, $4\frac{1}{2}$, 5 ...

This is how you count by **quarters**:

$\frac{1}{4}$, $\frac{2}{4}$, $\frac{3}{4}$, 1, $1\frac{1}{4}$, $1\frac{2}{4}$, $1\frac{3}{4}$, 2, $2\frac{1}{4}$, $2\frac{2}{4}$, $2\frac{3}{4}$, 3 ...

This is how you count by **eighths**:

$\frac{1}{8}$, $\frac{2}{8}$, $\frac{3}{8}$, $\frac{4}{8}$, $\frac{5}{8}$, $\frac{6}{8}$, $\frac{7}{8}$, 1, $1\frac{1}{8}$, $1\frac{2}{8}$, $1\frac{3}{8}$, $1\frac{4}{8}$,

$1\frac{5}{8}$, $1\frac{6}{8}$, $1\frac{7}{8}$, 2, $2\frac{1}{8}$ ...

Fraction wall for halves, quarters & eighths

Equivalent fractions are exactly the same size, even though they are made up of different size pieces.

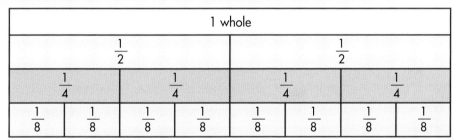

1 whole							
$\frac{1}{2}$				$\frac{1}{2}$			
$\frac{1}{4}$		$\frac{1}{4}$		$\frac{1}{4}$		$\frac{1}{4}$	
$\frac{1}{8}$	$\frac{1}{8}$	$\frac{1}{8}$	$\frac{1}{8}$	$\frac{1}{8}$	$\frac{1}{8}$	$\frac{1}{8}$	$\frac{1}{8}$

Equivalent fractions might look like this if you use 8 objects.

1 group of 8

2 groups of 4

4 groups of 2

8 groups of 1

 Try this

1 $\frac{2}{8}$ is the same size as _____

2 $\frac{1}{2}$ is the same size as _____ or _____

3 $\frac{4}{4}$ is the same size as _____ or _____ or _____

FIFTHS, TENTHS AND HUNDREDTHS

Fifths

Fifths are 5 equal parts.

Each finger on one hand is a fifth.

$\dfrac{1}{5}$ $\dfrac{2}{5}$ $\dfrac{3}{5}$ $\dfrac{4}{5}$ $\dfrac{5}{5}$ $\qquad$ $\dfrac{5}{5}$ = 1 whole hand

10 ducks can be grouped into fifths.

$\dfrac{1}{5}$ of 10 = 2 $\quad$ $\dfrac{2}{5}$ of 10 = 4 $\quad$ $\dfrac{3}{5}$ of 10 = 6

$\dfrac{4}{5}$ of 10 = 8 $\quad$ $\dfrac{5}{5}$ of 10 = 10 $\quad$ $\dfrac{5}{5}$ = 1 whole group of 10 ducks

Tenths

If you divide each fifth into 2 equal parts, then you get tenths.

$\dfrac{1}{5}$

$\dfrac{2}{10}$

$\dfrac{1}{5} = \dfrac{2}{10}$

You can divide a set of 10 objects into $\frac{1}{10}$ s.

$\dfrac{1}{10}$ of 10 = 1 $\qquad$ $\dfrac{5}{10}$ of 10 = 5 $\qquad$ $\dfrac{9}{10}$ of 10 = 9

$\dfrac{2}{10}$ of 10 = 2 $\qquad$ $\dfrac{6}{10}$ of 10 = 6 $\qquad$ $\dfrac{10}{10}$ of 10 = 10

$\dfrac{3}{10}$ of 10 = 3 $\qquad$ $\dfrac{7}{10}$ of 10 = 7 $\qquad$ $\dfrac{10}{10}$ =

$\dfrac{4}{10}$ of 10 = 4 $\qquad$ $\dfrac{8}{10}$ of 10 = 8 $\qquad$ 1 whole pile of strawberries

$\dfrac{1}{10}$

Hundredths

If you divide each tenth into 10 equal parts, then you get hundredths.

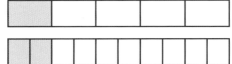

$\dfrac{1}{100}$ is one tenth of $\dfrac{1}{10}$

$\dfrac{1}{10} = \dfrac{10}{100}$ $\qquad$ $\dfrac{100}{100} = 1$

Here are some fractions for $100.

$\dfrac{1}{5}$ of \$100 = \$20 $\qquad$ $\dfrac{1}{10}$ of \$100 = \$10 $\qquad$ $\dfrac{1}{100}$ of \$100 = \$1

DECIMALS

Decimals are special fractions. They are always divided into 10 or 100 equal parts, or any other **power of 10**. Decimals are part of our base 10 counting system.

It is important to listen carefully when using **tens** or ten**ths**, or **hundreds** and hundred**ths**. The 'th' lets you know it is a decimal fraction. Decimals are another way to write tenths and hundredths.

Decimal is the Latin word for 'a tenth part'.

You **measure using decimals**.

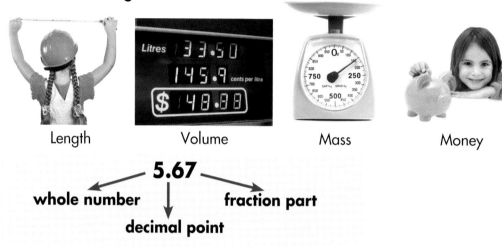

| Length | Volume | Mass | Money |

5.67

whole number   **fraction part**

decimal point

- You use a **decimal point** to show that you are writing decimals.
- If you have a whole number, then it goes to the left of the decimal point.
- Fractions go to the right of the decimal point.
- You read this decimal point symbol as '**and**'.
- The whole number and the decimal fraction add together to make the number.

You can write decimal numbers on a place value chart.

thousands	hundreds	tens	ones	and	tenths	hundredths
1000s	100s	10s	1s	•	$\frac{1}{10}$ s	$\frac{1}{100}$ s
			4	•	7	

4.7 is 'four and seven tenths'	40 tenths and 7 tenths = $\frac{47}{10}$
4 is the same number as $\frac{40}{10}$	4.7 is the same number as 47 tenths.

DECIMALS (continued)

If there are no whole numbers, you just say the decimal fraction.

0.45 is 'forty-five hundredths' or 'four tenths and 5 hundredths'

thousands	hundreds	tens	ones	and	tenths	hundredths
1000s	100s	10s	1s	•	$\frac{1}{10}$ s	$\frac{1}{100}$ s
			0	•	4	5

Numbers to the **right** of the decimal point are always 10 times smaller. Numbers to the **left** of the decimal point are always 10 times larger.

ORDERING DECIMALS

You put decimals in order by size.

1. If the whole number is larger, then that number is larger.

$5.07 is more than $3.99 because the whole number 5 is larger than the whole number 3.

2. If there are no whole numbers, then the larger decimal fraction is the largest number.

$0.95 is larger than $0.85

Some people think a large fraction is a long decimal number.

They think 0.19 must be larger than 0.2 because it is longer. It looks bigger.

This is true if it is a whole number. But you need to look at the place value.

a. Which number, 0.19 or 0.2, has the larger tenths value?

2 tenths are larger than 1 tenth

b. If there are no tenths, which number has the larger hundredths value?

Which is larger: 0.02 m or 0.03 m?

3 cm is longer than 2 cm

3 hundredths are larger than 2 hundredths

3. You can put more than two decimal numbers in order by size.

| 4.7 kg | 0.58 kg | 6.36 kg | 0.19 kg |

The best strategy is to write them in a place value chart.

tens	ones	and	tenths	hundredths
10s	1s	•	$\frac{1}{10}$ s	$\frac{1}{100}$ s
	4	•	7	0
	0	•	5	8
	6	•	3	6
	0	•	1	9

You can add a **0** to the hundredths place in the first number so that all the spaces are the same. You can now compare sizes starting at the left.

Look down the 1s column, 6 is the largest so 6.36 is the largest number. The next largest decimal is 4.7.

That leaves 0.58 and 0.19. Look down the tenths column. 5 is larger than 1 so 0.58 is larger than 0.19.

Circle the larger number in the pair.

1 5.88 or 6.1   **3** 2 or 1.08

2 0.99 or 1.0   **4** 32.1 or 9.87

Try this

MONEY

Decimal currency means your money is divided up into 10s and 100s.

Russia used the first decimal currency over 300 years ago.

1 rouble = 100 kopecks

Australia has used decimal currency since 1966.

One billion coins were needed to change over from the old Imperial money to the new Australian dollars and cents.

$1 COIN

Our money is based on 100 cents or one golden coin called a dollar.

$1 = 100 cents

	Designer	Colour	Front picture	Mass	Diameter	Thickness
$1	Stuart Devlin	gold	kangaroos	9 g	25 mm	3 mm

To convert dollars to cents multiply by 100.

$6 = 6 × 100c = 600 cents

To convert cents to dollars divide by 100.

800 cents   800 ÷ 100 = $8

To find out how many more cents you need to make the next dollar just add up to the next 100. Try to do this quickly in your head.

30c + 70c = $1   20c + 80c = $1
55c + 45c = $1   48c + 52c = $1

Every time you get 100 cents you get another $1. Try to do this quickly in your head too.

$1.60 + 40c = $2 $3.70 + 30c = $4
$9.80 + 20c = $10 $4.90 + 10c = $5

$2 COIN

2 × $1 = $2

Over 20 000 000 $2 coins are minted each year.

	Designer	Colour	Front picture	Mass	Diameter	Thickness
$2	Horst Hahne	gold	Aboriginal hunter	6.6 g	20.5 mm	3.2 mm

The dollar is divided up into 4 smaller units:
5 cents, 10 cents, 20 cents and 50 cents.

Any amount less than $1 is a decimal fraction.

Decimals are a special way to write tenths and hundredths.

The Royal Australian Mint produces about 2 million coins each day.

5-CENT COIN

	Designer	Colour	Front picture	Mass	Diameter	Thickness
5 cents	Stuart Devlin	silver	echidna	2.83 g	19.41 mm	1.3 mm

5 cents = five hundredths of a dollar
= 5/100 of a dollar
= $0.05
= 5c
There are twenty 5c coins in $1 so 5c is also $\frac{1}{20}$ of a dollar.

If you buy 10 blocks for 5 cents each, how much change will you get from $1?

10 × 5c = 50c $1 − 50c = 50c

So, you will get 50c change from $1.

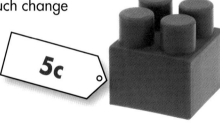

5c

10-CENT COIN

10 cents	Designer	Colour	Front picture	Mass	Diameter	Thickness
	Stuart Devlin	silver	lyre bird	5.65 g	23.6 mm	2 mm

10 cents = ten hundredths of a dollar
= 10/100 of a dollar
= 1/10 of a dollar
= $0.10
= 10c
There are ten 10c coins in $1.

If you buy 8 lemons for 10 cents each, how much change will you get from $2?

8 × 10c = 80c, so you need 20c more to make $1

Then, you need another $1 to make $2.

You will get $1.20 change altogether.

20-CENT COIN

20 cents	Designer	Colour	Front picture	Mass	Diameter	Thickness
	Stuart Devlin	silver	platypus	11.3 g	28.52 mm	2.5 mm

20 cents = twenty hundredths of a dollar
= 20/100 of a dollar
= $0.20
= 20c
There are five 20c coins in $1 so 20c is $\frac{1}{5}$ of a dollar.

If you buy 6 gingerbread biscuits for 20 cents each, how much change will you get from $5?

6 × 20c = 120c

That is, $1.20.

So, you need another 80c to take you to $2.

And, you need $3 more to take you to $5.

You will get $3.80 change altogether.

20c each

50-CENT COIN

50 cents	Designer	Colour	Front picture	Mass	Diameter	Thickness
	Stuart Devlin	silver	kangaroo and emu	15.55 g	31.51 mm	2 mm

Fifty cents is the largest Australian coin. It has 12 straight sides. It is shaped like a dodecagon.

50 cents = fifty hundredths of a dollar
= 50/100 of a dollar
= $0.50
= 50c
There are two 50c coins in $1 so it is $\frac{1}{2}$ of a dollar.

In 2007, Canada minted the largest coin in the world, a gold coin worth $1 000 000. It has a mass of 100 kg, a diameter of 50 cm and a thickness of 30 mm.

If you buy 7 eggs for 50 cents each, how much change will you get from $10?

7 × 50 = 7 × 5 × 10

= 35 × 10

= 350 cents or $3.50

50c each

You need 50c more to take you to $4.

And, you need $6 more to take you to $10.

You will get $6.50 change altogether.

$5, $10, $20, $50 & $100 NOTES

Australia was the first country to produce plastic bank notes rather than paper notes. Plastic notes last longer and are more difficult to copy illegally.

$ Notes	Designer	Colour	Length mm	Width mm	Front	Back
$5	Bruce Stewart	mauve	130	65	Parliament House	Queen Elizabeth II
$10	Max Robinson	blue	137	65	Banjo Paterson	Dame Mary Gilmore
$20	Garry Emery	red	144	65	Mary Reibey	John Flynn
$50	Brian Sadgrove	yellow	151	65	David Unaipon	Edith Cowan
$100	Bruce Stewart	green	158	65	Dame Nellie Melba	General Sir John Monash

$78.95

If you buy one pair of shoes, how much change will you get from $100?

It is easier to add up to $100.

5 more cents takes you to $79

$21 more takes you to $100

So, you will get $21.05 change.

Try this

If you have one of each coin, how much is that altogether? $_____

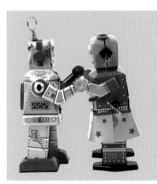

Challenge

These toys cost $45.75. How much is that in:

1 5-cent coins?
2 10-cent coins?
3 20-cent coins?
4 50-cent coins?

PATTERNS & ALGEBRA

NUMBER SENTENCES

Mathematics has sentences too. Instead of words you use numbers and symbols to tell your story. You can express a number problem in words, a drawing or a model. We use a number sentence to work out our problem.

If you are **adding**, it does not matter which number goes first in your sentence.

26 + 198 or 198 + 26

Both answers are the same, 224.

If you are **subtracting**, it does matter which number goes first in your sentence.

374 – 96 is not the same as 96 – 374

The answers are **not** the same.

If you are **multiplying**, it does not matter which number goes first in your sentence.

56 × 10 or 10 × 56

Both answers are the same, 560.

If you are **dividing**, it does matter which number goes first in your sentence.

700 ÷ 10 is not the same as 10 ÷ 700

The answers are **not** the same.

Each number matches part of your real life problem.

Ali has 9 fish tanks. There are 8 fish in each tank.

He has another small tank with 5 fish and a small bowl with 1 goldfish.

9 × 8 + 5 + 1 = 76

Try this

NUMBER SENTENCES (continued)

Which is the matching number sentence?

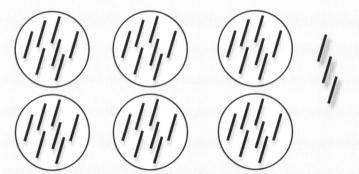

$7 \times 3 + 6 = 27$
$6 \times 7 + 3 = 45$
$3 \times 6 + 7 = 25$
$6 + 7 + 3 = 16$

FINDING MISSING NUMBERS

Remember numbers can have many names.

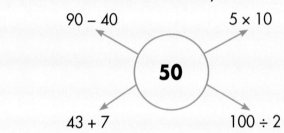

$90 - 40$ 5×10

50

$43 + 7$ $100 \div 2$

This can help you solve tricky problems.

Gran gave Jack $23 and $19. She gave Mia $50. How much does Mia owe Gran if the amounts should be the same?

You can record this problem as a number sentence with one number missing.

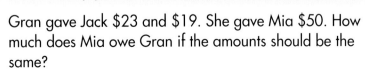

23 + 19 = 50 – □ or 50 – □ = 23 + 19

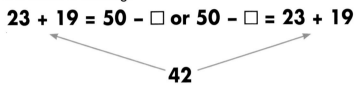

42

This problem is now saying 42 is the same number as $50 - \square$.

That is easy to do in your head

50 – 8 leaves 42, so □ must be 8

Mia needs to pay Grandma back $8.

NUMBER PATTERNS

Patterns are all around you. When you have a pattern, you can describe it to a friend, see how it continues and predict what the next part will be.

What is the next shape in the pattern? A circle

Numbers also make patterns. You add, subtract, multiply or divide to create a sequence of numbers you can describe, continue and predict.

7, 9, 25, 3, 100 is not a number pattern.

You cannot describe it. You cannot continue it. You cannot predict what the next number will be.

CREATING A PATTERN RULE

To make a number pattern you need a rule.

Your rule lets you predict what the next number will be.

4, 8, 12, 16, 20, 24, 28 ...

You are **adding 4** each time.

The next number in this pattern is **32**.

You continue this pattern by adding 4 to the last number.

A number pattern can start at any number.

39, 32, 25, 18, 11 ...

You are **taking away 7** each time.

The next number in this pattern is **4**.

You always continue this pattern by taking away 7 from the last number. Sometimes that takes you into negative numbers!

CREATING A PATTERN RULE (continued)

Patterns in a list or table

You can write **patterns in a list**.

1
1 + 2 = 3
1 + 2 + 3 = 6
1 + 2 + 3 + 4 = 10
1 + 2 + 3 + 4 + 5 = 15

You can write **patterns using a mix of operations**.

$(1 \times 1) + 1 = 2$
$(2 \times 2) + 2 = 6$
$(3 \times 3) + 3 = 12$
$(4 \times 4) + 4 = 20$

You can write **patterns in a table**.

Step 1	$(1 \times 1) + 1$	1 + 1	2	
Step 2	$(2 \times 2) + 2$	4 + 2	6	+ 4
Step 3	$(3 \times 3) + 3$	9 + 3	12	+ 6
Step 4	$(4 \times 4) + 4$	16 + 4	20	+ 8
Step 5				
Step 6				
Step 7				

Lists and tables help you think about the pattern.

Even if you cannot describe it easily in words, you can see that for Step 5 you will write
$(5 \times 5) + 5 = 25 + 5 = 30$.

Try this

Write in the steps 5, 6 and 7 in the table above.

Mathematicians like to find a way to predict any number in a pattern.

Can you discover a rule to predict what the 8th step will look like?

What will the 9th step look like?

Look at Step 4. It was $(4 \times 4) + 4$.

You can predict that Step 10 will be $(10 \times 10) + 10$.

A rule is like magic. It reveals the number for you.

OTHER INTERESTING NUMBER PATTERNS

Triangular numbers

You need a pile of blocks or counters. Make the smallest triangle shape you can. Record how many you use.

This number sequence shows you how many counters you need if you keep making larger triangles by adding a new layer like this:

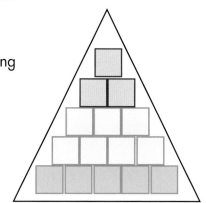

1
1 + 2 = 3
1 + 2 + 3 = 6
1 + 2 + 3 + 4 = 10
1 + 2 + 3 + 4 + 5 = 15

**1, 3, 6, 10, 15, 21, 28, 36, 45 ...
are triangular numbers.**

You can use different colours to make the pattern stand out. You can continue this pattern forever.

A French man called Blaise Pascal explored this pattern over 350 years ago. He discovered so many hidden patterns within it that it is now called Pascal's Triangle.

Square numbers

You need a pile of blocks or counters. Make the smallest square shape you can. Record how many you use. Keep increasing the length of each side.

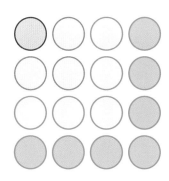

This number sequence shows you how many counters you need if you keep making larger squares like this.

Notice that you are adding the next odd number each time. Patterns help you predict. If you added 7, then you can predict you will add 9 to make the next square.

1 + 3 = 4
1 + 3 + 5 = 9
1 + 3 + 5 + 7 = 16
1 + 3 + 5 + 7 + 9 = 25

4, 9, 16, 25, 36, 49 ... are square numbers

If you add odd numbers in counting order, then you always get a square number. You can always find a way to rearrange this many objects to make a square.

LENGTH

Humans love to measure and compare lengths. A length measurement is the distance between the start and the end of the thing being measured.

There are over 100 different words to help you talk about length.

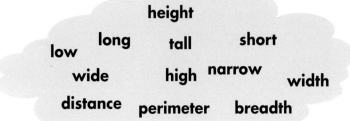

height
low long tall short
wide high narrow width
distance perimeter breadth

You measure length by dividing the thing you want to measure into equal size, smaller lengths called **units**. You use a ruler or a tape measure to help you do this. You measure lengths like your height, how far you can throw a ball, how high you can jump.

Since 1983, mathematicians and scientists define a metre as the length travelled by light in a vacuum in 1/299 792 458 of a second.

METRE

Australia uses metric units. These were first used in France in 1799. The standard metric unit for measuring length is a **metre**. It comes from a Greek word metron, which means 'measure'.

The symbol for a metre is **m**.

⊢——— 5m ———⊣

Find a tape measure. Where does a metre come to on your body if you start at your feet? Where does it come to if you hold your hands out and start at one fingertip? Use this body measure to help you remember what a metre length looks like.

Try this

Challenge

If you stand at your front door, where will 10 m away be? Where will 20 m away be? Where will 50 m away be? How can you check?

CENTIMETRE

Lengths shorter than a metre can be measured in short, equal length units called **centimetres**.

One unit is this long: ____

The symbol for a centimetre is **cm**.

If you divide a metre into 100 equal length parts, a centimetre is the length of one of these parts. The prefix centi means one hundredth.

The Great Pyramid in Giza, Egypt, was built by ancient Egyptians using the cubit as a length measure. A cubit was about 53 cm long. It was a measure from the elbow to the fingertip.

There are 100 centimetres in a metre.	**100 cm = 1 m**
A centimetre is 1 hundredth of a metre.	**1 cm = $\frac{1}{100}$ m**

Centimetres can be written as a decimal number too.

    1 cm   = 0.01 m
    10 cm = 0.1 m or 0.10 m
    50 cm = 0.5 m or 0.50 m

You can say 4.5 m as '4 metres and 5 tenths of a metre'.

You can say 2.68 m as 'two metres and sixty-eight hundredths of a metre'.

All of these lines are exactly 10 cm long.

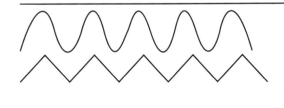

15 cm

Use a ruler to measure the length of your hand.
Where does 10 cm come to? Use this body measure to help you remember what 10 cm looks like.

Try this

Challenge
Close your eyes. Think of something in the room that is exactly 25 cm long. Think of something that is 50 cm long. Think of something that is 80 cm long. How can you check?

CALIBRATIONS

When you look at a ruler or a tape measure, not all the numbers are shown. You have to work out what each marking means. These marks are called **calibrations**.

This pencil ends at the 6.7 cm mark.

Each **number marks** the length of **10 mm** or 1.0 cm

The **longer marks** measure **5 mm** or 0.5 cm.

Each of the **tiny marks** measure **1 mm** or 0.1 cm.

Make your own centimetre tape measure.

Try this

- Cut a 1 m strip of paper.
- Fold it in half. Mark the fold as 50 cm.
- Fold it again to find and mark 25 cm and 75 cm.
- Use a ruler to mark 10 cm lengths all along your tape.
- Draw a mark for each cm.

Use this to practise measuring lengths until you are accurate.

MEASURING IN TWO DIMENSIONS

You can measure length in more than one dimension. If you measure the sides of an oblong, you need to measure not just **how wide** it is but also **how long** it is. This is measuring in two dimensions (2D).

width or breadth

length

Most people say that the width is always the shorter side and the length is the longer side.

Perimeter is the special word meaning the total length of all the sides of a 2D shape.

To measure the perimeter of this house fence you would need to measure each side of the fence, not just the front fence.

The perimeter of this fence is 4 + 4 + 1 + 8 + 2 + 8 + 1 + 4 = 32 m.

Start
measuring
here

You can record length measurements in metres (m)
and centimetres (cm).

These two lines are both 16 cm long.

16 cm is the same as 0.16 m or 16 tenths of a metre.

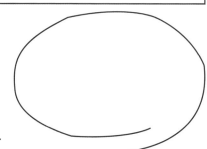

If a length is longer than a metre, you can still record
your measurement using m and cm.

The length of this old bike is

162 cm

1 m and 62 cm

1.62 m

Bicycle.

The average height of an adult woman is about 166 cm.
The average height of an adult man is about 179 cm.
How tall are you?
Use a tape measure to find your height in centimetres.
Record your height in three different ways.

Try this

MEASURING IN THREE DIMENSIONS

Sometimes you want to know **how long**, **how high**
and **how deep** an object is. This is a measurement in
three dimensions (3D).

Will this box fit onto a shelf that is 40 cm high?

length = 71 cm

height = 42 cm

depth = 35 cm

This box is 2 cm too high to fit the shelf.

But if you turn it on its side it will fit.

MOVING
DAY

MILLIMETRES

Very short lengths can be measured in very short, equal length units called **millimetres**.

The symbol for a millimetre is **mm**.

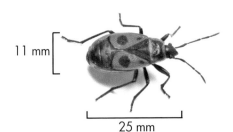

11 mm

25 mm

If you divide one metre into 1000 equal length parts, a millimetre is the length of one of these parts. The prefix milli means one thousandth.

There are 1000 mm in a metre.
 1000 mm = 1 m
A millimetre is 1 thousandth of a metre.

$$1 \text{ mm} = \frac{1}{1000} \text{ m} \qquad 100 \text{ mm} = \frac{1}{10} \text{ m}$$

$$10 \text{ mm} = \frac{1}{100} \text{ m}$$

Millimetres can be written as a decimal number too.

1 mm = 0.001 m
10 mm = 0.010 m
100 mm = 0.100 m

You can say 1.005 m as 'one metre and five thousandths of a metre'.

You can say 5.068 m as 'five metres and sixty-eight thousandths of a metre'.

Use a ruler to measure the width of a finger.

Can you find a finger that is exactly 10 mm wide? Use this body measure to help you remember what 10 mm looks like.

Try this

Challenge

Look around you. Find something that is 30 mm long.
Find something that is 60 mm long.
Find something that is 90 mm long.
How can you check?

Accuracy with millimetres

Measuring lengths in millimetres is very accurate. Most builders measure lengths in millimetres. Builders talk about 'mills'.

There are 10 millimetres in 1 centimetre.
10 mm = 1 cm

A millimetre is $\frac{1}{10}$ of a centimetre.

$1 \text{ mm} = \frac{1}{10} \text{ cm}$ $1 \text{ mm} = 0.1 \text{ cm}$ $5 \text{ mm} = 0.5 \text{ cm}$

MIXING LENGTH UNITS

You can record measurements longer than a metre in either millimetres or metres and centimetres.

This crocodile is 3080 mm long.

That is the same as:
3 m and 8 cm
3.080 m long
3 and 80 thousandths of a metre

TIPS ABOUT MEASURING LENGTH

Straight lengths are easy to measure.

To estimate:

• you imagine each unit being repeated along the length you are measuring

• you divide each unit in proportion (relate the sizes to each other) in your mind

You can use a straight wooden or plastic ruler to check your estimate. Find the starting point 0 on your ruler. Make sure you place this part of the ruler at the start of your line.

On this tape, 0 starts here.

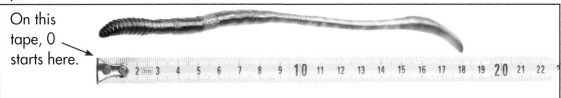

This worm is about 18 cm or 180 mm long.

The Caribbean thread snake is the shortest snake in the world. It is about 100 mm long, which is 0.1 m long. The SE Asian reticulated python is the longest snake in the world. It is about 10 m long. That's 100 times longer than a thread snake!

TIPS ABOUT MEASURING LENGTH (continued)

Crooked or wiggly lengths are not easy to measure. To estimate you still imagine each unit being repeated along the length you are measuring. You still divide it up in proportion in your mind.

You can use a flexible tape measure to check your estimate.

Find the starting point 0 on your tape measure. Make sure you put this part of the tape at the start of your line.

You always start at 0 to measure. If you just place your ruler or tape measure anywhere, you will get the wrong measurement.

This is not where 0 starts

This pencil is not 20 cm long.

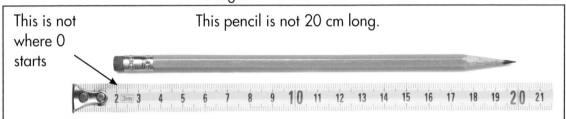

Remember that some lengths join up to the start again.

Perimeter is the total length around the outside of a 2D shape.

You call the length around the outside of a circle the circumference.

Sometimes you cannot reach a length to measure it.

You have to find something closer.

For example: the length of a ceiling is the same as the length of the wall along the floor.

If you compare lengths, do not get confused by the numbers.

Think about what each length really looks like.

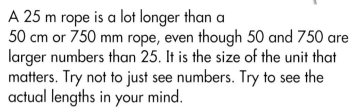

This flower is 16.5 cm high.
16 mm is too small.
16 m is too large.

A 25 m rope is a lot longer than a 50 cm or 750 mm rope, even though 50 and 750 are larger numbers than 25. It is the size of the unit that matters. Try not to just see numbers. Try to see the actual lengths in your mind.

You know that 1 m is a lot longer than 1 cm. You need 100 cm before you get the same length as just 1 m.

An easy way to compare lengths is to make all the measurements the same unit.

1 m = 100 cm

> Ten metres is 10 times larger than 1 m.
> 10 m = 10 × 100 cm = 1000 cm

To work out how many centimetres in a metre you multiply by 100.

1 m = 1000 mm

So, you need 1000 mm before you get the same length as a 1 m.

> Six metres is 6 times 1000 mm.
> 6 m = 6 × 1000 mm = 6000 mm

To work out how many millimetres in a metre you multiply by 1000.

The world's smallest submarine is 2.95 m long.
Find different ways to record this length in mm, cm and m.

Try this

AREA

Area is a measure of the space inside a two-dimensional boundary.

Irregular hexagon

Television screen

You measure flat areas like bedroom floors, walls or ceilings; material to make a tent; wrapping paper to cover a box or the space taken up by a play area.

Here are a few words to help you talk about area.

wide

covers more than

large

small

covers less than

narrow

SQUARE METRES

You measure area by dividing what you want to measure into equal size, square units.

The standard metric unit for measuring large, flat areas is the **square metre**. The symbol for a square metre is **m²**.

The little 2 is a short way of saying m × m.

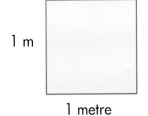

1 m

1 metre

1 m × 1 m = 1 m²

The area of this basketball court is 28 m × 15 m = 420 m².

As **one square metre** is quite large, you can draw it as a small square when you are recording areas.

Even though the unit is called a square metre, the shape does not have to stay a square.

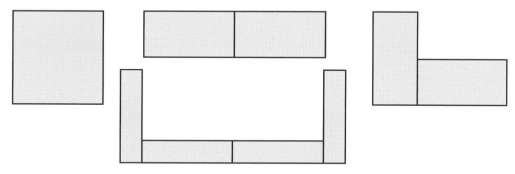

These shapes all have the same area. In real-life they can be rearranged to make one square metre of area.

ESTIMATING AREA

To estimate area rearrange parts of an area in your mind to see how many square metres you can make. Keep all the proportions the same.

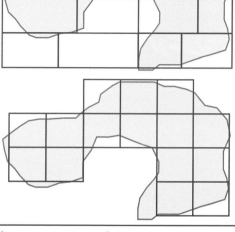

This is not a good area estimate.

This is a good area estimate.

You can use rulers, tape measures and square unit grids to measure area.

MEASURING RECTANGULAR AREAS

To measure rectangular areas imagine rows of square metres to fill the space you want to measure.

To find the area of a wall imagine square metres end-to-end, then row by row.

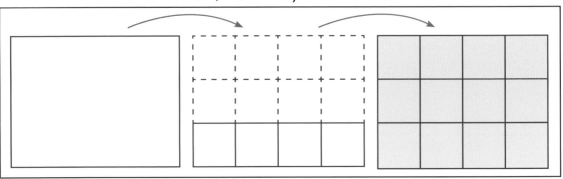

The area of this wall is **4 + 4 + 4 = 12 m^2**

that is **3 m × 4 m = 12 m^2**

One litre of paint covers about 16 m^2.

If you want to do two coats of paint on this wall, then you need to buy 2 L of paint.

One of the largest shopping mall areas in the world is in Beijing, China. It covers about 659 600 square metres.

USING A CALCULATOR TO FIND AREA

Multiplication is a fast way to calculate areas. You can use a tape measure to find how many m^2 units fit the width. You can then measure how many rows of m^2 fit your area. When you multiply these two numbers, you get the area measure quickly without having to count each square metre.

This garden measures

12 m × 4.5 m.

It has an area of 54 m^2.

Use a tape measure and some masking tape.
Mark out 1 square metre of area on some concrete. Close your eyes and try to see the size of this area in your mind.

Imagine 2 m^2, imagine 4 m^2, imagine 10 m^2

What different shapes could they be?

Try this

SQUARE CENTIMETRES

Small flat areas can be measured in units called **square centimetres**.

The symbol for a square centimetre is **cm²**.

1 square centimetre

The area of this shape is 5 cm².

Even though this unit is called a square centimetre, the shape does not have to stay a square.

These shapes all have an area of 1cm².

They can be rearranged to make one square centimetre of area.

AREAS OF 100 cm²

Imagine one square metre divided up into a grid with 10 rows and 10 columns. Each grid space has an area of 100 cm².

Remember that areas can be any shape. So, 100 cm² can be any shape too.

Draw your own 100 cm² grid. Use a ruler to measure and mark ten 1 cm columns on a piece of paper. Use a ruler to measure and mark ten 1 cm rows across these columns. You now have horizontal and vertical grid lines marking out 100 cm².
Use this grid to help you measure small, flat 2D areas.

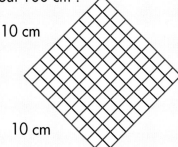

10 cm

10 cm

The green square on this page is exactly 100 cm².

This yellow rectangle has an area of exactly 100 cm².

Try this

Try this

AREAS OF 100 cm² (continued)

Count how many square units are covered.

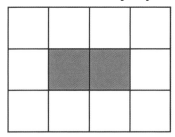

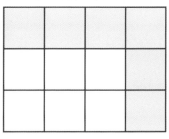

_____ square units   _____ square units

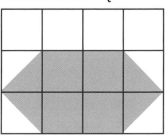

_____ square units

ESTIMATING MESSY AREAS

Some areas are not neat and tidy.

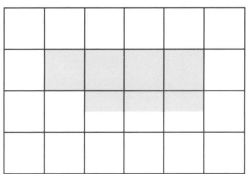

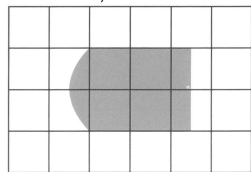

And some areas are really messy.

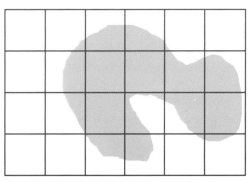

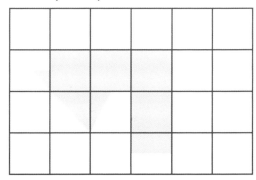

If you cannot draw the area on a cm² grid, then you need to imagine putting a transparent grid on top of each area.

It is difficult to measure messy areas exactly. Estimate by counting any square units that are completely covered by the grid. Next imagine joining up extra bits until they cover one unit on the grid. Keep doing this in your mind. Keep counting units as you go.

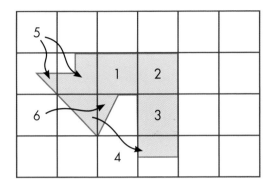

The area of this shape is a bit bigger than 5 cm².

COMPARING AREAS

Areas are only large or small when you compare them. On their own they are just an area. But as most areas are a different shape and size, it can be difficult to work out which area is larger than another.

Which is larger, your hand print or your foot print?

How can you find out? Try using your eyes first. Does one area look larger than the other? If they are both close in size, you could trace the outlines onto paper and then cut them out. Cut one of the outlines into parts and then match the parts to the other outline. Which is larger?

If you need to know the exact area in cm², then you need to use the grid method.

An inch is an old length measure. People think it came from measuring the distance from your thumb joint to the top of your thumb.

1 inch _____

An 'elephant' was a piece of paper 23 inches wide and 28 inches long. That is about $\frac{4}{10}$ of a square metre.

SURFACE AREAS

Some areas are not 2D shapes.

Three-dimensional (3D) objects have **surface area** on the outside.

- An orange has a curved surface area of orange peel around it.

- A box has six flat faces creating its surface area.

- Your skin has a surface area.

An average newborn baby is covered by 0.25 m² of skin.

These surface areas are all difficult to measure.

One way to measure surface area is to flatten out a 3D object and then try to find the area of the new 2D shape.

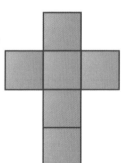

- You can peel an orange and see what it covers in square centimetres.

- You can flatten a box, measure the area of each flat face and then add up all your measurements.

An average nine-year-old child is covered by 1.07 m² of skin.

But you cannot flatten everything. You need to estimate some surface areas such as:

- the number of square metres needed to re-cover the lounge

- the number of square metres of skin on your body.

An average adult is covered by 1.73 m² of skin.

MASS

Mass is a measure of the heaviness of an object.

It is a measure of how much 'stuff' there is in an object; how much matter the object contains. A little bit feels light and a lot feels heavy.

You measure the mass of shopping items, parcels, cooking ingredients or your own mass. When you go shopping, you can divide up all your items into different bags so that one bag is not too heavy to carry.

You pay more to post a heavy parcel than a light parcel.

Ancient humans measured mass using grains of wheat or barley for very light objects and large stones for heavy objects.

Objects are only heavy or light when you compare them. A small pebble is heavier than a small leaf, but the same small pebble is much lighter than a book.

You **heft** to compare two masses by holding them in each hand to feel the mass. One mass will feel lighter than, the same as or heavier than the other.

Here are a few words to help you talk about mass.

light

heavy

heft

mass

find the mass of

lift

USING A MASS BALANCE DEVICE

You can measure mass using:

- an equal-arm balance
- a rocker balance

A balance using stones was first invented by humans over 4000 years ago. All over the world, symbols of justice often show someone holding up an equal-arm mass balance.

- a kitchen scale
- a bathroom scale.

When you put objects onto a balancing device, the scale tells you whether the objects are the same mass, lighter than or heavier than each other.

The pig is heavier than the ball.	The pig is the same mass as the ball.	The pig is lighter than the ball.

KILOGRAMS

The original world standard for a kilogram is a metal cylinder kept in a vault near Paris, France.

You measure mass using equal size units.

The standard metric unit for measuring mass is the **kilogram**.

One kilogram always has a mass of 1 kilogram, even if it is feathers.

The symbol for a kilogram is **kg**.

A 10 × 10 × 10 cm cube of water has a mass of 1 kg.
One litre of pure water has a mass of 1 kg.
Meat is measured in kilograms.
Fruit and vegetables are measured in kilograms.

Objects you measure will have masses more than 1 kg,
equal to 1 kg or less than 1 kg.

The world's largest
gold nugget was
found in Victoria in
1869. It has a mass
of about 71 kg.

Heaviness of 1 kg

1 Find a kitchen scale. Put a 1 kg bag of flour or sugar
on the scale.

2 Check the measurement. It should read 1 kg.

3 Pick up the bag and hold it in one hand. Close your
eyes. Try to remember what this 1 kg mass feels like.

Try this

GRAMS

Plenty of things are much lighter than 1 kg.

If you divide a 1 kg mass into one thousand smaller
parts, a **gram** is the mass of one of these parts. You use
grams to measure the mass of objects lighter than 1 kg.

The symbol for a gram is g.

There are 1000 g in 1 kilogram.

$$500 \text{ g} = \frac{1}{2} \text{ kg}$$

$$250 \text{ g} = \frac{1}{4} \text{ kg}$$

$$100 \text{ g} = \frac{1}{10} \text{ kg}$$

$$1 \text{ g} = \frac{1}{1000} \text{ kg}$$

The world's
heaviest pumpkin
had a mass of about
821 kg and was
grown in Minnesota,
USA, in 2010.

GRAMS (continued)

You can use a variety of small masses to measure light objects.

Try this

This egg has a mass of 60 g.

Masses

1 Use play dough or plasticine to make your own small masses.

2 Use a kitchen scale to measure each lump.

3 Make some lumps 10 g and some lumps 100 g.

4 You can make heavier masses by filling empty containers with sand and putting the lid on. Try 200 g or 500 g.

5 Label your masses.

Mixing mass units

You record masses using either kilograms, grams or both.

A small baby has a mass of 2150 g.

2150 g is the same as 2 kg and 150 g or 2.15 kg.

In words it is 'two kilograms and fifteen hundredths of a kilogram'.

CALIBRATIONS

Mass scales can be in a straight line but many are curved.

When you look at a mass scale, not all the numbers are shown. You have to work out what each mark means. These marks are called calibrations.

On this scale, there are 9 marks between 90 and 100 kg.

Each mark measures 1 kg.

ORDERING MASSES

Some people think that a very large object must always be heavier than a very small object. But mass has nothing to do with the volume or size of an object. Mass measures the heaviness of an object.

A very small object can be heavier than a very large object. Two objects that are the same size do not necessarily have the same mass. You have to heft or measure using scales to check. Just looking at them is not good enough.

This is full. It has a mass of 360 g.

This is empty. It has a mass of 10 g.

To put two or more masses in order of heaviness:

* heft to see if the difference is really obvious
* measure exactly using a balance scale and smaller masses
* order the written masses.

The mass of Lucy's three cakes are 1.45 kg, 750 g and 1100 g.

Put them in order from lightest to heaviest.

Remember to make all the units the same size before you compare.

Try this

WHAT ABOUT WEIGHT?

People use the word 'weight' when they refer to mass. The correct way to talk about mass is to say 'find the mass of ...' or 'this mass is as heavy as ...' or 'my mass is 43 kg'.

Weight is a science measurement. It is a measure of the effect of the earth's gravity pulling down on your mass. It is measured in units called Newtons. You will learn more about weight in secondary school.

If you could travel to the moon, then your mass would be exactly the same as on earth. But your weight would only be $\frac{1}{6}$ what it is on earth. The moon's gravity has a much lighter pull on our mass.

In outer space, your mass would be exactly the same as on earth, but you would have no weight as there is no gravity pulling on you.

VOLUME & CAPACITY

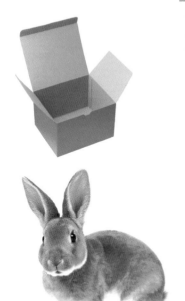

Volume is a measure of how much three-dimensional (3D) space an object takes up. Volume does not measure heaviness.

The volume of this box is the same whether it is empty or full.

People also use the word volume when they talk about sound, books and traffic.

You compare volumes by seeing which 3D object takes up more space than another. It is obvious a rabbit takes up more space than a mouse.

Capacity measures the maximum volume inside a container. How much can it hold? It is a three-dimensional measure. But not everything is a container with empty spaces inside that can be filled up. Boxes, cans and bottles can hold different volumes. A rock cannot hold anything inside it because it does not have an empty space.

Here are some words to help you talk about volume and capacity.

amount

almost full   empty half full

full   small   container

overflowing   large

CUBIC METRES

You measure volume and capacity by dividing what you want to measure into equal size smaller units.

The standard metric unit for measuring volume and capacity is the **cubic metre**. This is quite large. One cubic metre takes up as much space as a 1 x 1 x 1 m cube.
The symbol for one cubic metre is **m³**

You will learn more about this in the Year 5 and 6 Maths Guide.

LITRES

The **litre** is a smaller unit for measuring how much space a liquid takes up or how much liquid a container can hold.

The symbol for a litre is **L**. A litre takes up the same space as a 10 × 10 × 10 cm cube.

1 litre of milk   1 litre of paint

Many everyday objects are measured in litres.

Your mum has about 4.5 litres of blood in her body.

This bottle holds 2 L of detergent.

This bucket holds 10 L of water.

The petrol tank in this car holds about 60 L.

Challenge

A litre of liquid can be any shape. It does not have to look like a cube. Measure out exactly 1 L of water. In a variety of different containers, try to predict where 1 L of water will come up to on the side. Try to remember these different proportions.

This skill will help you estimate litres better.

MILLILITRES

You use a very small unit called a **millilitre** to measure very small amounts of liquid.

The symbol for a millilitre is **mL**.

One millilitre of water takes up as much space as 1 cubic centimetre.

There are 1000 millilitres in 1 litre.

$$1 \text{ mL} = \frac{1}{1000} \text{ L}$$

You can use small measuring spoons or even plastic syringes to measure liquids in millilitres.

$$1000 \text{ mL} = 1 \text{ L}$$
$$500 \text{ mL} = \frac{1}{2} \text{ L}$$
$$250 \text{ mL} = \frac{1}{4} \text{ L}$$
$$100 \text{ mL} = \frac{1}{10} \text{ L}$$

Old capacity measures were based on a cubic inch.

A tablespoon has a capacity of 1 cubic inch. A cup has a capacity of about 15 cubic inches. You still use tablespoons and cups as measures of capacity today.

1 teaspoon holds 5 mL of medicine.

This bottle holds 500 mL of shampoo.

Try this

Estimating litres

To estimate litres you divide the amounts into units in your mind. Find five different containers in your home. Estimate their capacity and find a way to check. Sort them by capacity from the least to the most.

VOLUME & CAPACITY CALIBRATIONS

You use marked containers to measure litres and millilitres. These marks are calibrations. But when you look at a measuring jug or a bucket, not all the numbers are shown. Sometimes not even the marks are shown. You have to work it out using proportional reasoning.

Each mark on this bucket measures 1L.

Each mark on this medicine jar measures 5 mL.

Each mark on this jar measures 50 mL.

This shows you the 900 mL mark

This shows you the 100 mL mark

Make your own volume and capacity measurer.

1 You need an empty, transparent, large bottle, a 1 L jug, a 100 mL small cup and a waterproof marker pen.

2 Over a sink, fill the 100 mL cup with water and pour it into the bottle.

3 Draw a mark on the bottle where the water reaches.

4 Do this 10 times. The 10th mark will be your 1 L mark.

5 Pour out the water from your bottle into the known 1L container.

6 Do they match? Use your home-made, litre measurer to practise measuring capacities until you are very accurate.

Try this

MEASURING VOLUME BY COUNTING CUBES

Curved volume units, like balls, have too many empty spaces between them.

Boxes of different sizes stack but there are still plenty of gaps and empty spaces.

To measure volume more accurately you need a unit with no gaps when you stack units together. Cubes stack with no gaps and no overlaps. Cubes are a more accurate unit for measuring volume.

This object is made from 8 cubes.

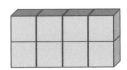

4 cubes are on the top layer
4 cubes are on the bottom layer

Some 3D objects have the same volume. You can rearrange the same number of volume units to make objects with different shapes. Sometimes the blocks are hidden from view when viewing from some angles.

The volume of each object is 8 cubes.

Hidden
block behind
this one

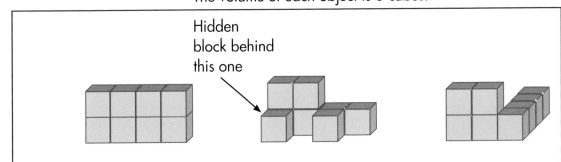

Sometimes you need to imagine what the volume units are, even though they are not there. You imagine dividing the object up in your mind.

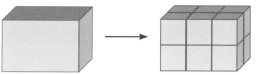 This block has a volume of 12 cubes

Try this

Counting cubes

If 1 unit looks like this , what is the volume of each of these objects?

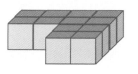

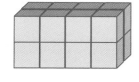

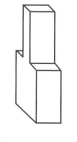

_____ cubes   _____ cubes   _____ cubes

COUNTING MISSING BLOCKS

Sometimes you see a box that is not full yet. You use proportional reasoning to work out how many more units you need to fill the box.

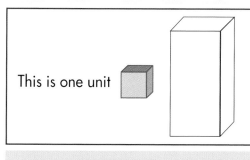

This is one unit

The bottom layer can have 4 units. There is one missing

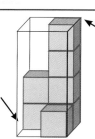

There are 4 layers. That's 4 + 4 + 4 + 4 or 4 × 4 = 16 blocks altogether.

Challenge

How many blue blocks should there be altogether in this rectangular prism?

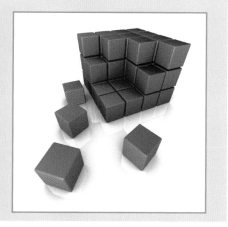

_____ blue blocks

CUBIC CENTIMETRES

Very small capacities can be measured in very small units called **cubic centimetres**.

The symbol for a cubic centimetre is **cm³**.

The small 3 is a symbol for 3 dimensions
1 × 1 × 1 cm.

This is 1 cubic centimetre.

You use cubic centimetres to measure volumes and capacities that are not liquids.

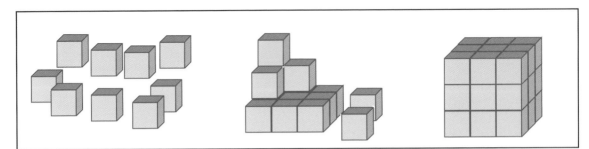

This cube is made from 3 layers of 9 cubic centimetres.

That's 9 + 9 + 9 cubic centimetres.

That's 3 × 9 = 27 cubic centimetres.

You estimate volume by imagining an object cut up into cubic centimetres.

Even though the unit is called a cubic centimetre, the shape does not have to stay a cube.

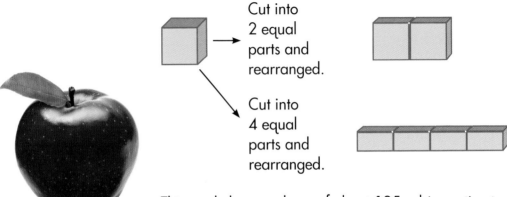

Cut into
2 equal
parts and
rearranged.

Cut into
4 equal
parts and
rearranged.

This apple has a volume of about 125 cubic centimetres.

TIME

Time is a funny thing. You cannot see it but you can experience time passing. If you look very carefully, you can see a shadow move across a wall. This is time passing as the earth rotates towards the east.

There are many words to help you talk about time.

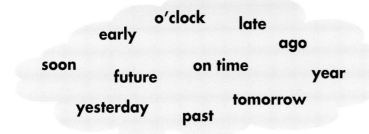

o'clock
late
early
ago
soon
on time
future
year
yesterday
tomorrow
past

You use time measurements every day. You need to wake up on time. You need to cook your toast for only a short time or it will burn. You need to catch the bus so you are not late for school. You look forward to your birthday. You remember something good that happened in the past.

HOURS

One full day's rotation of planet Earth is divided into 24 equal parts called **hours**. People have tried all sorts of ways to measure the length of one hour.

Using an egg timer

Using a sundial

Your hair grows about 1 cm every 20 days.

The world's largest sundial was built in Jaipur, India, about 1730.

HOURS (continued)

In one hour, you can cook 1 kg lamb at 180°C or walk about 4 km.

The symbol for 1 hour is h.

You measure hours passing with a clock.

Try this

Time passing

Set an alarm clock to go off in 1 hour. Try to feel the time passing. Think about what you can do in that time.

How many pages of a book can you read?

How far can you walk?

am is short for ante meridiem (before midday)

pm is short for post meridiem (after midday)

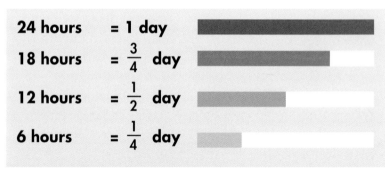

24 hours	= 1 day
18 hours	= $\frac{3}{4}$ day
12 hours	= $\frac{1}{2}$ day
6 hours	= $\frac{1}{4}$ day

MIDNIGHT & MIDDAY

Most people think of 24 hours as 2 groups of 12 hours.

Most people think of 12 hours as a circle, not a straight line.

The circle is a symbol of time as a cycle that repeats forever.

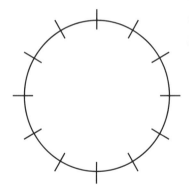

Midnight is 12:00. It is the end of a day.

Midday is also 12:00. It is halfway through a day.

am is time measured before midday.

pm is time measured after midday.

MINUTES

People wanted a shorter measure of time. They thought an hour was too long.

A **minute** is one sixtieth of an hour.

60 minutes = 1 hour

45 minutes = $\frac{3}{4}$ hour

30 minutes = $\frac{1}{2}$ hour

15 minutes = $\frac{1}{4}$ hour

The symbol for 1 minute is min.

In one minute, you can put on your shoes and socks, cook a slice of toast or read a page in a book.

You can measure minutes passing using a kitchen timer, the seconds hand on a wristwatch or a stopwatch.

You look at the dial and set it to the number of minutes you need. You use proportional reasoning to work out what time each mark means.

Use a minute measurer to see how long a minute feels.
If you have a bell on your timer, close your eyes and open them when the bell rings.

Other things you might measure in minutes:

- a shower takes about 3 minutes.
- cupcakes take about 20 minutes to bake.

There are 24 × 60 minutes in one day, which is 1440 minutes.

Try this

Don Maclurcan walked across Australia in 67 days, 2 hours and 57 minutes in 2002.

In Australia, one baby is born every 1 minute and 45 seconds.

SECONDS

People wanted a smaller measure of time passing than a minute.

A **second** is one sixtieth of one minute.

60 seconds = 1 minute

30 seconds = half a minute

The symbol for 1 second is s.

In one second, you can blink your eye, flick your finger or say the word 'one'.

Try this

Use a stopwatch to see how long 10, 20 and then 30 seconds feels.

You measure seconds passing using the seconds hand on a wristwatch or a stopwatch.

You look at the dial and set it to the number of seconds you need.

There are 60 × 60 seconds in one hour, which is 360 seconds.

You need to use proportional reasoning to work out what each mark means.

ANALOGUE CLOCKS

Our word 'clock' comes from a Dutch word for bell. The first mechanical clocks were invented about 700 years ago. An **analogue clock** has a round face divided into 12 equal parts. Each part represents one hour passing. It measures time using angles.

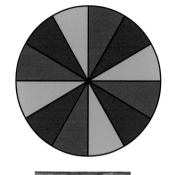

There are many different types of analogue clocks.

wall clock   wristwatch   town clock

Most clocks have numbers in a circle from 1 to 12.

Some clocks have Roman numerals.

The funny thing is you do not need all the numbers.

In fact, you do not need any numbers at all.

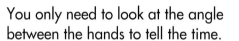

You only need to look at the angle between the hands to tell the time.

Analogue clocks use two or three hands to show the time angle. The shorter hand shows the hour. The longer hand shows the minutes. Sometimes there is a third hand that shows the seconds passing.

Try this

ANALOGUE CLOCKS
(continued)

On the hour, the hour hand points to the number of the hour. The minute hand always points to the 12.

10 o'clock

Write the time shown on each clock.

__ o'clock __ o'clock __ o'clock __ o'clock __ o'clock __ o'clock

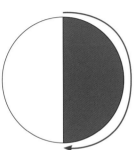

30 minutes

Half past

30 minutes is half an hour. On the half hour, the hour hand points halfway past the previous hour. The minute hand moves halfway around the clock to the 6.

You say: **half past twelve**

You write: **12:30**

You can also read it as two numbers: **twelve thirty**

Try this

What is the time for each clock? Write it as you would say it, write it and read it.

Quarter past

15 minutes is a quarter of an hour. At quarter past, the minute hand moves to the 3 to show one quarter of a circle.

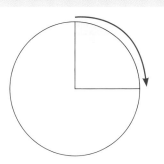

You say: **fifteen minutes past eight**

You write: **8:15**

You can also read it as two numbers: **eight fifteen**

What is the time for each clock?
Write it as you would say it, write it and read it.

Quarter to

45 minutes is three quarters past the last hour. Quarter to is 15 minutes before the next hour. The minute hand moves to the 9 to show three quarters of a circle.

Try this

You say: **forty-five minutes past six** or **fifteen minutes to seven** or **a quarter to seven**

You write: **6:45**

You can also read it as two numbers: **six forty-five**

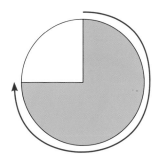

ANALOGUE CLOCKS (continued)

What is the time for each clock?
Write it as you would say it, write it and read it.

Try this

Reading time to the nearest minute

The small marks around the clock face show 60 minutes.

Look at what hour number the hour hand has gone past.

Use proportional reasoning to work out where the minute hand is pointing.

Try this

The hour hand has gone past the ten and the minute hand is 8 minutes (marks) past the 12.

You say: **eight minutes past ten**

You write: **10:08**

You can also read it as two numbers: **ten-o-eight**

8 minutes past 10

What is the time for each clock?
Write it as you would say it, write it and read it.

DIGITAL CLOCKS

Digital time is easy to read because **digital clocks** measure time using numbers not angles.

Most digital clocks show 12 hours and minutes.

The left hand numbers show the hours passing. They show 0 for time between midnight and 1 o'clock. They then show all the numbers from 1 to 12 in order.

The right hand numbers show the minutes. They show 00 for o'clock and then all the numbers from 01 to 59 in order.

There is usually a small am or pm symbol in the top left of the clock to show times before and after midday.

You say or read it as:
ten forty-five or
15 minutes to 11

You write: **10:45**

Look at this watch.

Record the time in as many ways as you can.

Try this

Scientists think it will take up to 50 000 years for a plastic container to decompose.

Try this

SOLVING TIME PROBLEMS

How many hours in 2 days and 3 hours?

> Work out how many groups of 24 hours you have.
> $2 \times 24 = 48$ hours
> Don't forget to add the extra 3 hours.
> $48 + 3 = 51$ hours

How many hours in 75 minutes?

> Work out how many groups of 60 minutes you have.
> $75 = 60 + 15$
> So you have 1 hour and 15 minutes.

How many seconds in 3 minutes and 15 seconds?

> Work out how many groups of 60 seconds you have.
> $3 \times 60 = 180$ seconds
> Don't forget to add the extra 15 seconds.
> $180 + 15 = 195$ seconds

Solve the following time problems

1 How many hours in 90 minutes?

2 How many minutes in 3 hours and 5 minutes?

3 How many seconds in 2 minutes and 11 seconds?

OTHER USEFUL TIME FACTS

7 days	**= 1 week**
2 weeks	**= 1 fortnight**
4 weeks	**= 1 month**
12 months	**= 1 year**
365 days	**= 1 year**
366 days	**= 1 leap year**

The life cycle of a butterfly is about 42 days.

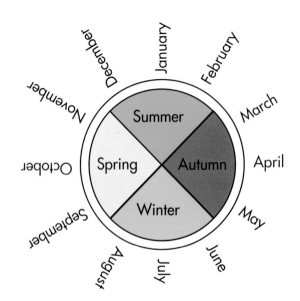

CALENDAR

Calendars help you plan your time.

They show each of the 12 months of a year in order from January to December.

They show the number of days in each month.

You say the numbers as position words like first, second and third.

The days are in groups of 7 to show the weeks, starting with Sunday.

The first day of the month follows the last day of the month before.

Some days are left blank at the start and finish of a calendar.

A calendar has rows and columns to help you work out the **date**.

You look along the rows to see each week.

You look down the columns to see the same day of the week.

We are going camping on Friday 25 November.

Try this

Look at this calendar for April.

1 How many days in April?

2 How many Fridays in April?

3 What is the date of the first Sunday?

4 Which day is three days before Tuesday 19 April ?

5 Which day comes after 23 April ?

6 Which day is the third Friday?

TIMETABLES

Timetables help you know when to catch transport. They show you when your favourite TV program starts. They tell you when a movie starts. They are packed full of information.

Daily Ferry Timetable

Departs	Time					
Wharf 1	9:00 am	10:30 am	11:45 am	1:30 pm	3:00 pm	4:45 pm

Try this

If you miss the 9:00 am ferry you have to wait $1\frac{1}{2}$ hours until the next one.

The 3rd ferry leaves at 11:45 am.

There are no more ferries leaving after 4:45 pm.

There is one ferry leaving between 12:00 and 2:00 pm.

Write four things you know after reading this movie timetable.

Orion Cinema Timetable

Movie	Monday	Wednesday	Friday	Saturday
Mighty Ming	10:00 am	1:30 pm	12:15 pm	11:00 am
The Best Day of My Life	12:30 pm	4:45 pm	2:45 pm	1:00 pm
Tex and Rex in Mex	3:00 pm	7:00 pm	4:30 pm	3:30 pm

TIMELINES

Timelines are number lines with significant dates in order starting with the earliest date. You can record family events in years or show the growth of a plant in weeks. You decide the length of your timeline, and then you put your dates in order. The lines can be straight or curved. Use proportional reasoning to place each date on the timeline.

Reaching Space First

1957 1st satellite

1959 1st spacecraft to moon

1961 1st man in space

1963 1st woman in space

1965 1st space walk

1969 1st man on moon

1971 1st space station

1981 1st space shuttle

1957 1959 1961 1963 1965   1969 1971   1981

TEMPERATURE

Temperature is a measure of how hot or cold something is. You measure temperature using scaled units called **degrees Celsius**. You write everyday temperatures using the symbol **°C**. The tiny circle stands for 'degrees'. The capital C stands for the first letter in the name Celsius. You always leave a space between the number and the °C symbol.

If someone is angry, they are in a temper or 'hot'.

Celsius was a famous Swedish astronomer who developed temperature scales. He lived over 250 years ago.

In January 1960, the temperature was 50.7 °C at Oodnadatta, SA

Using a version of his scales, 0 °C is the temperature when water freezes and 100 °C is the temperature when water boils.

Sometimes people also say 'degrees centigrade' when talking about temperature. This is the original name used by Celsius himself. It is Latin for 100 steps, like the 100 degrees between 0 and 100.

Thermometers

A **thermometer** is a device that helps you measure temperature. It has a special coloured liquid inside, which expands or goes up when it is hot. The liquid contracts or goes down when it is cool.

There are many different types of thermometers to measure temperature.

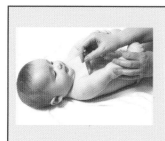

The temperature of the sun is about 6.5 million °C.

TEMPERATURE (continued)

Using temperature

Hot things can be dangerous, so you usually see them marked red such as the hot tap in your kitchen, bathroom or laundry. You need to take extra care near hot objects.

You wear clothes based on temperature. Most people think that it is a very hot day if the temperature reaches 30 °C or more. On hot days, you wear light clothes to keep your body temperature cool.

Most people think it is a very cold day if the temperature drops below 15 °C. On cold days, you rug up and wear hats, gloves, jumpers and scarves to keep your body temperature warm.

The normal body temperature of a human is about 37 °C.

The normal body temperature of a dog is a little bit hotter at 38 °C.

The normal body temperature of a budgerigar is hotter still at 41 °C.

You use temperature every day if you cook. A cake is baked in an oven at about 165 °C. If you cook it in a cooler oven, it will not bake properly and might be soggy. If you bake it in a hotter oven, it might burn. Most ovens have a built-in thermometer so you can see when the temperature is just right.

Match the temperatures to the pictures.

1

2

39 °C

0 °C

170 °C

3

4

−10 °C

TEMPERATURE CALIBRATIONS

When you look at the markings on a thermometer not all the lines are numbered.

You use proportional reasoning to work out what number each mark represents.

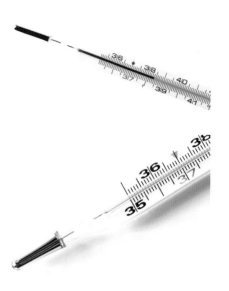

On this thermometer, there are ten small spaces between 36 and 37. Each small mark represents $\frac{1}{10}$ of a degree. The red arrow on the thermometer is pointing to 37 °C.

You write these numbers as decimals such as 36.1°C. You say thirty-six and $\frac{1}{10}$ of a degree. There are longer marks halfway between each number such as at 36.5 °C.

WEATHER FORECASTS

Meteorologists use maths and science to predict the weather each day. You find their predictions in the newspaper, on the radio, on TV and on the internet. Temperature predictions help you plan ahead. You might hang the washing out to dry or pack the correct clothes for a trip.

There are many different ways you can talk about weather temperatures.

- The **minimum** is the lowest or coldest temperature expected.
- The **maximum** is the highest or hottest temperature expected.
- The **range** is the difference between the highest and the lowest temperatures. You subtract the lowest from the highest temperature.
- A **minus** temperature is when it drops below 0 °C such as –5 °C.

Antarctica is the coldest place on earth. It can reach –89 °C.

The world's greatest temperature range 105 °C (–68 °C to 37 °C) was recorded in Siberia, Russia.

The world's hottest place is the Lut desert in Iran with 70.6 °C.

Try this

WEATHER FORECASTS (continued)

You find the **average** temperature for a week by adding up the seven daily temperatures and dividing by 7. You need these daily temperatures to be taken at the same time such as midday. You can put temperatures in order from the coolest to the warmest. You can investigate the extremes.

Predict the weather for the next 7 days. Record your prediction and the actual result. What is the difference between the coldest and the hottest temperature?

Challenge

Calculate the temperature range. Use this table to calculate your own temperature facts.

World Temperatures

Place	Minimum Yearly Temperature	Maximum Yearly Temperature	Temperature Range (Max – Min)	Average Temperature
Antarctica	–89 °C	15 °C		12.9 °C
Beijing, China	–10 °C	31 °C		11.8 °C
Cairo, Egypt	9 °C	35 °C		22 °C
Canberra, Australia	0 °C	28 °C		12.9 °C
Copenhagen, Denmark	–3 °C	22 °C		8.6 °C
Mexico City, Mexico	5 °C	27 °C		16.0 °C
Moscow, Russia	–14 °C	24 °C		4 °C
New Delhi, India	7 °C	41 °C		25.3 °C
Wellington, New Zealand	5 °C	20 °C		12.5 °C

3D OBJECTS

Three dimensional (3D) objects have width, height and depth. Most 3D objects are completely irregular with flat faces and bumpy surfaces. Their shapes are difficult to describe in words.

Some 3D objects can be talked about using mathematical words like spheres, prisms and pyramids.

Sphere

Prism

Pyramid

3D objects can be solid or empty. You still call them solids

When you can see through the faces, you see the **skeleton model**.

You can cut 3D shapes to reveal a **cross-section**.

These cuts can be at an angle or parallel to the base.

If your cut is parallel to the base, then the cross-section is the same shape as the base.

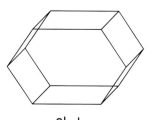

Skeleton

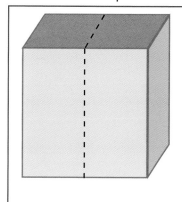 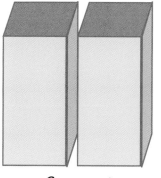 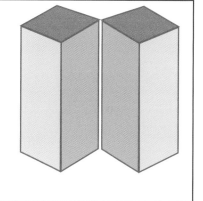

Cross-section

SPHERES

Spheres are completely round. There is no up or down. They are the same shape no matter which way you hold them. You often hear them called ball-shaped. Objects which look like a sphere are called spherical.

**Spheres have no flat faces.
They have no corners or vertices.
They have no straight edges.
They have just one curved surface.**

It is very difficult to flatten a sphere to make a 2D **net**.

A drawing of a sphere looks the same from every angle.

If you cut through the centre of a sphere, then the cross-section looks like this:

If you cut through anywhere else, then you get a smaller circle.

Half a sphere is called a **hemisphere**.

PRISMS

Prisms have flat faces with no curved surfaces. They have two identical (same shape and size) faces at the ends (or bases) and the faces that join up these two bases are parallelograms.

Prisms are useful as shapes for rooms or buildings. They are useful shapes for packages and containers. Food is sometimes cut into prisms

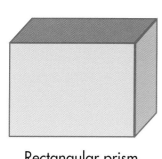
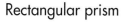

Rectangular prism   Hexagonal prism   Pentagonal prism

You name a prism by the shape of its base. The corners of a solid are called vertices.

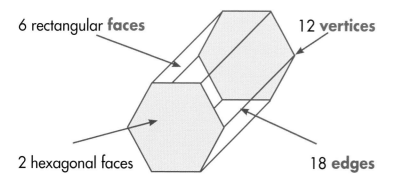

6 rectangular **faces**   12 **vertices**

2 hexagonal faces   18 **edges**

PRISMS (continued)

You can make a 3D model of a prism by drawing, cutting out then folding up a paper or cardboard net. Try to imagine flattening a prism to make a 2D net. There are many different ways to make a 2D net of a 3D prism.

Solid

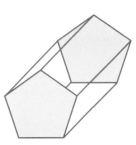

Net of solid

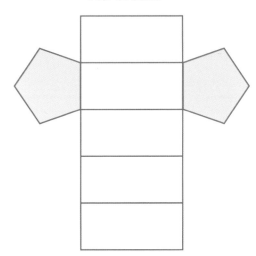

Triangular prisms

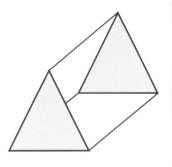

A triangular prism has 2 triangular bases.

It has 3 rectangular faces joining up the bases.

It has 5 flat faces altogether.

It has 6 vertices.

It has 9 straight edges.

Here is one way to **draw the net** of a triangular prism.

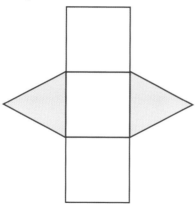

A drawing of a triangular prism looks different from **different viewing angles**.

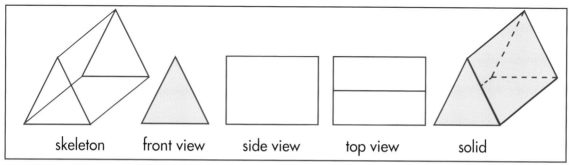

skeleton   front view   side view   top view   solid

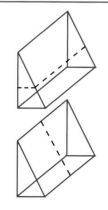

If you cut through the triangular prism like this, then you get this **cross-section**.

If you cut through the triangular prism like this, then you get this **cross-section**.

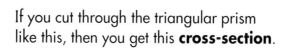

Cubes

Cubes (continued)

A **cube** is a square prism. It is a **regular** 3D solid. It is a **regular hexahedron**.

hexa = 6   hedron = face of a geometric solid

A square prism has 2 square bases the same shape and size at opposite ends and all other faces are rectangles.

A cube is a special square prism. It has every face the same shape and size. It has 4 square faces all the same size joining up the 2 square bases. If something is **cubical**, then it is shaped like a cube.

A cube has 6 flat square faces.
It has 8 vertices.
It has 12 straight edges.

There are 11 different nets for a cube.

Here are two different ways to **draw a net of** a cube.

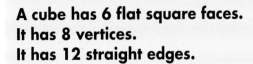

A drawing of a cube looks different from **different viewing angles**.

   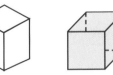

skeleton   front view   corner view   solid

   If you cut through a cube like this, you get this **cross-section**.

   If you cut through a cube like this, you get this **cross-section**.

OTHER PRISMS

Rectangular prism

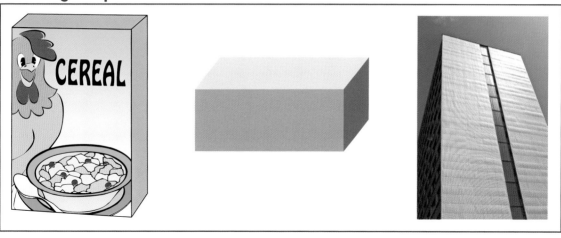

Pentagonal prism

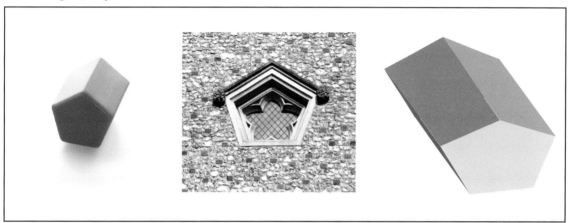

Hexagonal prism

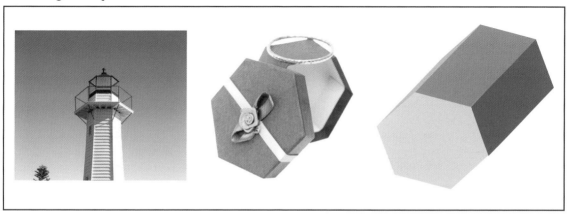

Octagonal prism

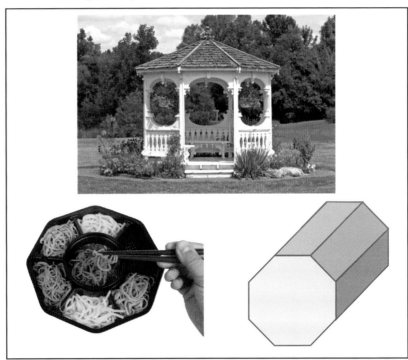

Prism	Base shape	Number of faces	Number of vertices	Number of edges
Rectangular	▭	6	8	12
Pentagonal	⬠	7	10	15
Hexagonal	⬡	8	12	18
Octagonal	⯃	10	16	24

Try this

Make a skeleton model of a prism

Use paddle-pop sticks and plasticine.

Or try to use matchsticks and play dough.

CYLINDERS

Anything to do with circles is always very special. A circular prism is so special you call it by another name, a **cylinder**.

A cylinder has circles as the 2 bases and one curved surface.

It has no vertex. It has two curved edges.

When you flatten a cylinder, it can look like this.

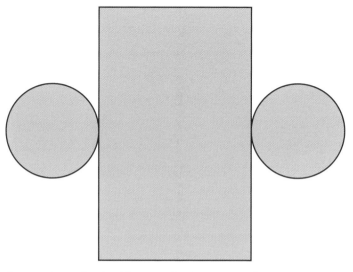

If something looks like a cylinder, even if it is not exact, you say it is **cylindrical**.

PYRAMIDS

For some reason people get mixed up when they think of the shape of pyramids and the shape of prisms. You need to see the picture of each one clearly in your mind.

Pyramids are not prisms. You describe pyramids by their base, just like prisms. But unlike prisms, pyramids have only one base. A triangular pyramid has one triangular base. A square pyramid has one square base.

Pyramids have triangular faces, not rectangular ones like prisms. These triangular faces always meet at one point, one **apex** or **vertex**.

The most famous pyramids in the world are in Egypt.

They were built over 4500 years ago. They stored the body of a dead king or pharaoh.

Pyramids are used in stacking, packing and building.

You can make a skeleton model of a pyramid using paddle-pop sticks and plasticine. Or you can try using matchsticks and play dough.

You can make a 3D model of a pyramid by drawing, cutting out and then folding up a net. There are many different ways to make a 2D net of a 3D pyramid.

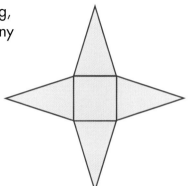

Triangular pyramids

A triangular pyramid has:

4 faces (1 triangular base and 3 more triangular faces)

4 vertices

6 straight edges

When you flatten a triangular pyramid, then the net can look like this.

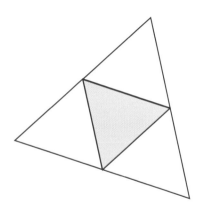

PYRAMIDS (continued)

A drawing of a triangular pyramid looks different from different viewing angles.

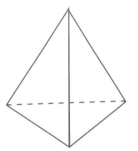

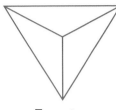

Top view

Side view

Triangular pyramids are all **tetrahedrons**. 'Tetra' means 4 and 'hedron' means face of a geometric solid. If all the triangles are equilateral, then it is a **regular tetrahedron**. All 4 faces are exactly the same shape and size.

Square pyramids

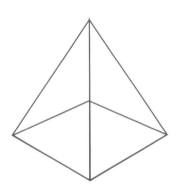

A square pyramid has:

5 faces (one square face and 4 triangular faces)

5 vertices

8 edges

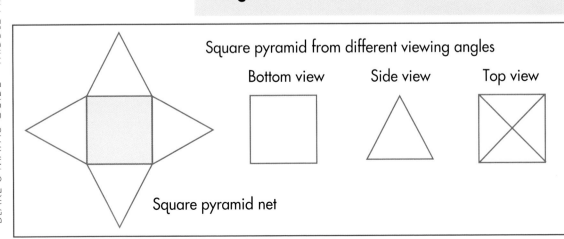

Square pyramid from different viewing angles

Bottom view · Side view · Top view

Square pyramid net

Rectangular pyramids

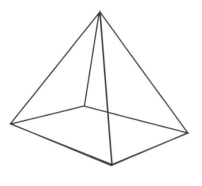
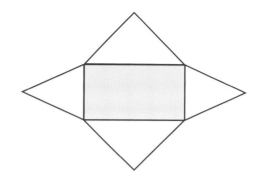

Rectangular pyramid from different viewing angles

Top view	Side view	Bottom view
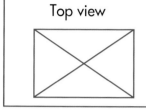		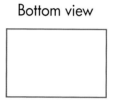

Pentagonal pyramids

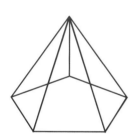

Pentagonal pyramid net

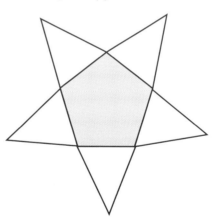

Pentagonal pyramid from different viewing angles

Top view	Bottom view	Side view
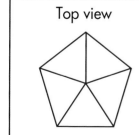	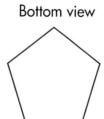	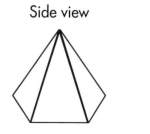

PYRAMIDS (continued)

Hexagonal pyramids

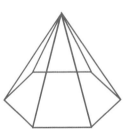

Hexagonal pyramid net

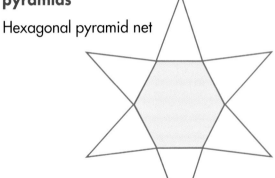

Octagonal pyramids

Octagonal pyramid net

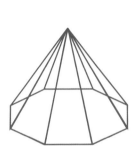

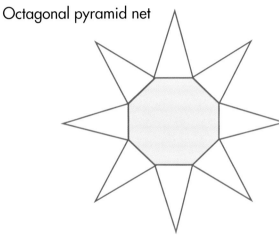

Pyramid	Base shape	Number of faces	Number of vertices	Number of edges
Rectangular		5	5	8
Pentagonal		6	6	10
Hexagonal		7	7	12
Octagonal		9	9	16

CONES

Anything to do with circles is always very special. A circular pyramid is so special you call it by another name, a **cone**.

A cone has a circle as the base and one curved surface. It has only one vertex or apex, the pointy bit of the cone.

Cones are very useful.

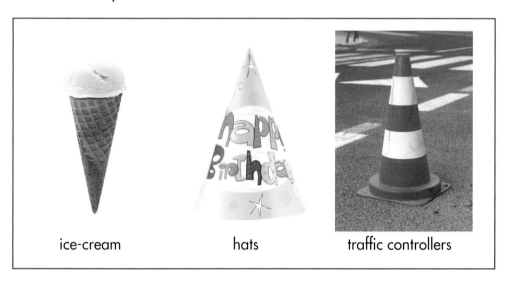

ice-cream   hats   traffic controllers

Net of a cone

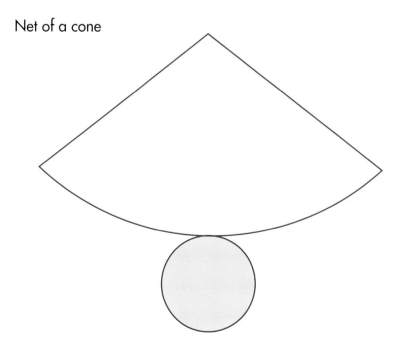

If something looks like a cone, even if it is not exact, you say it is **conical**.

2D SHAPES

Flat two-dimensional (2D) shapes are all around us.

They occupy the two dimensions of width and length.

They have no depth. They enclose an area of 2D space.

You see 2D shapes as faces of 3D objects. You see them as floors in a building or the front of the television.

If you can pick up a 2D shape, then it is really a 3D object. Even a thin sheet of paper has the third dimension of thickness. So when you sort objects in an activity you need to focus on the top surface only. Imagine the object has no thickness. Imagine it has only two dimensions. The 2D shape is the flat face.

You can trace, draw, cut out, bake or even use your body to create a 2D shape.

3D paint tin   2D circle

You sort, classify and talk about 2D shapes by:

- size (large, small)
- the shape of their sides (straight, curved, zigzag)
- the number of sides.

Polygons are 2D shapes with three or more straight sides and three or more angles.

poly = many   gon = corner

Polygons are named by old Greek or Latin counting words for the number of sides. **Regular polygons** have every side the same length and every angle the same size. Regular does not mean common or everyday.

STRAIGHT LINES FACT SHEET

Type of line	Drawing	Definition
horizontal		Lines that go from side to side, or left to right, parallel with the horizon or ground
vertical		Lines that go up and down at right angles to the ground
diagonal		A line that joins two corners that are not next to each other
parallel		Lines that never intersect and that are always the same distance from each other
perpendicular		Lines that meet at right angles
oblique		Lines that slant or slope but are not parallel, not diagonal, not horizontal and not vertical

Try this

STRAIGHT LINES FACT SHEET (continued)

Write the matching word to describe these straight lines.

1

_____ lines

2

_____ lines

3

_____ lines

Challenge

How many different straight lines can you discover in this picture ?

2D SHAPE OVERVIEW

Number of sides	Real life example	Name of shape	Irregular	Regular
1		circle		circle
			oval egg-shaped tear drop	
2		semi-circle		
3		triangle	scalene isosceles right-angled	equilateral
4		quadrilateral	trapezium parallelogram oblong rhombus	square

2D SHAPE OVERVIEW (continued)

Number of sides	Real life example	Name of shape	Irregular	Regular
5		pentagon	irregular pentagon	regular pentagon
6		hexagon	irregular hexagon	regular hexagon
7		septagon	irregular septagon	regular septagon
8		octagon	irregular octagon	regular octagon
9		nonagon	irregular nonagon	regular nonagon
10		decagon	irregular decagon	regular decagon

Circle fact sheet

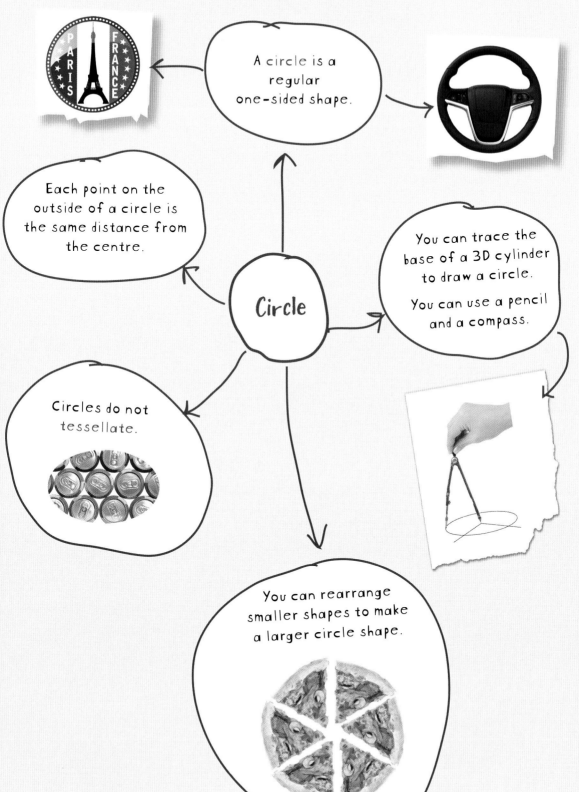

A circle is a regular one-sided shape.

Each point on the outside of a circle is the same distance from the centre.

Circle

You can trace the base of a 3D cylinder to draw a circle.

You can use a pencil and a compass.

Circles do not tessellate.

You can rearrange smaller shapes to make a larger circle shape.

Triangle fact sheet

GIVE WAY

tri = 3

- the sides can be any length
- three corners
- the corners can have any angle
- no curved sides

A polygon with 3 straight sides

Triangle

You can rearrange smaller shapes to make a larger triangle shape.

Regular triangle

If all the sides of a triangle are the same length, then it is an equilateral triangle. All the angles are exactly the same size.

An equilateral triangle is the only regular three-sided shape.

Quadrilaterals

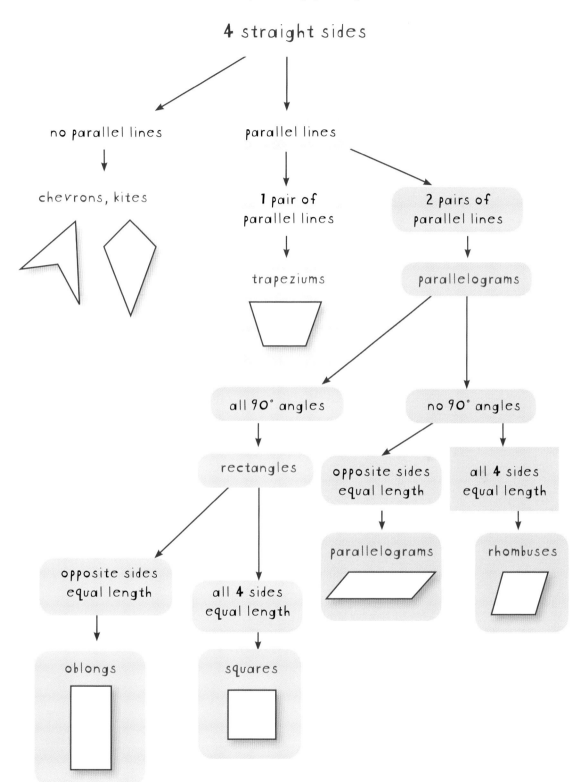

4 straight sides

no parallel lines → chevrons, kites

parallel lines

1 pair of parallel lines → trapeziums

2 pairs of parallel lines → parallelograms

all 90° angles → rectangles

no 90° angles

rectangles:
opposite sides equal length → oblongs
all 4 sides equal length → squares

no 90° angles:
opposite sides equal length → parallelograms
all 4 sides equal length → rhombuses

Rectangle fact sheet

- four straight sides
- quadrilateral
- two pairs of parallel sides
- oblongs and squares
- polygon
- closed shape with an inside area
- opposite sides equal length
- four right-angles (90°)

If all the sides of a rectangle are the same length, then it is a square.

A square is the only regular four-sided shape.

Rectangle

A square can be placed in any direction.

You can rearrange smaller shapes to make a square.

You can draw a square using a pencil, a set square and a ruler.

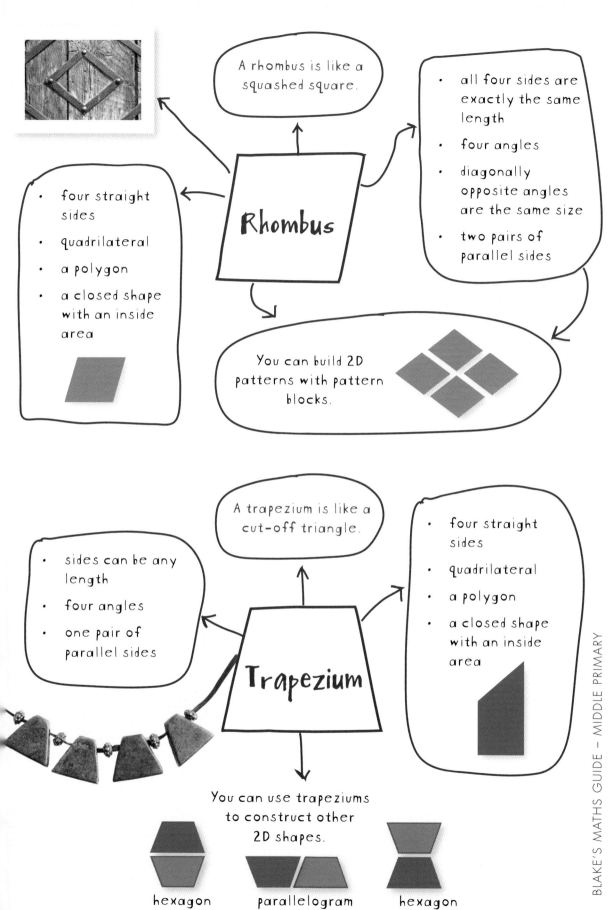

A rhombus is like a squashed square.

Rhombus

- all four sides are exactly the same length
- four angles
- diagonally opposite angles are the same size
- two pairs of parallel sides

- four straight sides
- quadrilateral
- a polygon
- a closed shape with an inside area

You can build 2D patterns with pattern blocks.

A trapezium is like a cut-off triangle.

Trapezium

- sides can be any length
- four angles
- one pair of parallel sides

- four straight sides
- quadrilateral
- a polygon
- a closed shape with an inside area

You can use trapeziums to construct other 2D shapes.

hexagon   parallelogram   hexagon

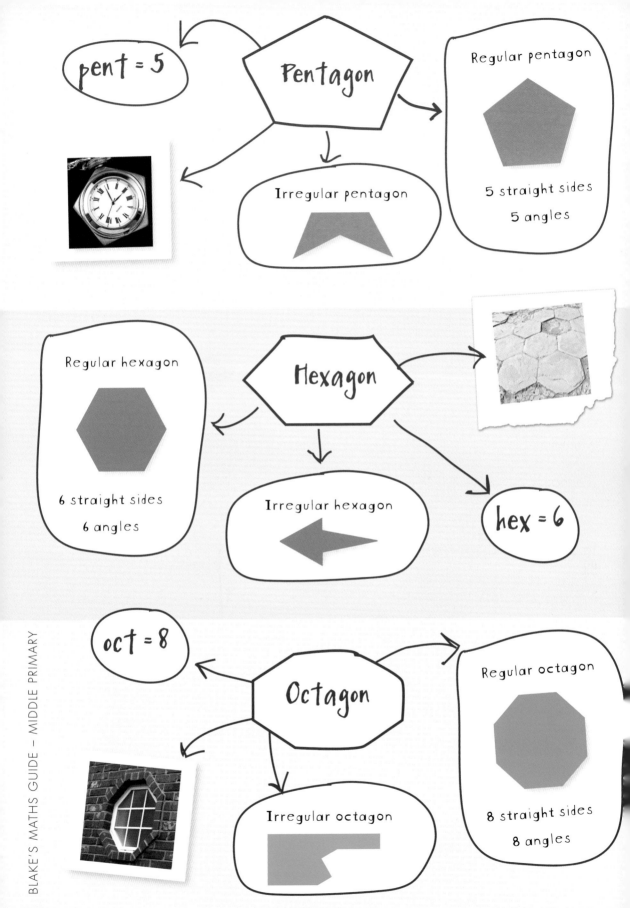

pent = 5

Pentagon

Regular pentagon

5 straight sides

5 angles

Irregular pentagon

Regular hexagon

Hexagon

6 straight sides

6 angles

Irregular hexagon

hex = 6

oct = 8

Octagon

Regular octagon

8 straight sides

8 angles

Irregular octagon

SYMMETRY

The word symmetry comes from an old Greek word meaning to measure together.

A symmetrical shape has an imagined line of symmetry that creates a mirror image or flip. It creates a reflection.

If a shape is symmetrical, then you can imagine folding it up and matching the two parts exactly.

Lots of people get confused about what symmetry means. They think that if you just cut something in half, then the two pieces will always be symmetrical.

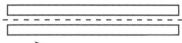

This is a line of symmetry

The top half of this rectangle is reflected exactly in the bottom half. The two pieces are symmetrical. The whole rectangle is symmetrical.

This is a mirror image of the top shape

To be symmetrical you need an exact mirror image or flip.

But sometimes even though the area is equal, the two shapes are not symmetrical. A line can cut a shape into two equal-size parts but still not be a line of symmetry.

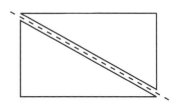

To find out if a shape is symmetrical, imagine drawing a line down the centre of the shape. If you find one line of symmetry keep looking to see if there are any others.

This is NOT a line of symmetry

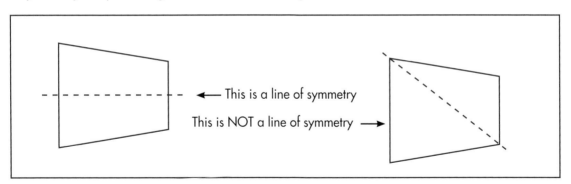

This is a line of symmetry

This is NOT a line of symmetry →

SYMMETRY (continued)

If you cannot find any lines of symmetry, then the shape is **not symmetrical**.

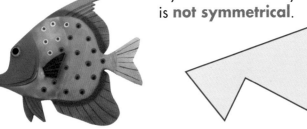
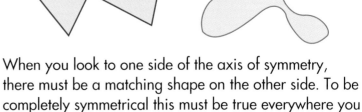

When you look to one side of the axis of symmetry, there must be a matching shape on the other side. To be completely symmetrical this must be true everywhere you look on either side of this imaginary line.

A 2D shape can be symmetrical.

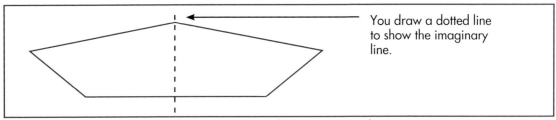

You draw a dotted line to show the imaginary line.

A pattern can be symmetrical.

There can be more than one line of symmetry.

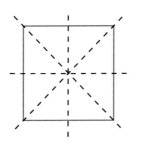

This square has four lines of symmetry.

A 3D object can be symmetrical.

You need to imagine cutting the object into two equal shape parts.

Try this

Draw the line of symmetry

Draw any lines of symmetry you spot in these 2D shapes.

 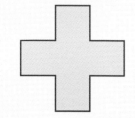 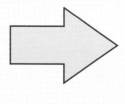

Draw any lines of symmetry you spot in each of these 3D shapes.

Challenge

How many lines of symmetry on this square pyramid?

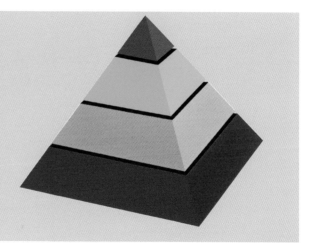

ANGLES

You see angles everywhere around you.

Openings create angles.

Slopes create angles.

Turns create angles.

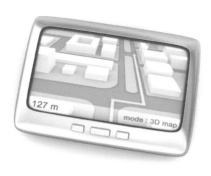 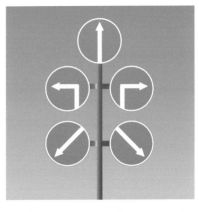

Angles are a measure of how far something has turned, opened or sloped.

Our word, angle, comes from an old Latin word for corner, but remember the corner is not the angle. If two straight lines, called arms or **rays**, meet at a corner, point or **vertex**, the angle is created by measuring the amount of turn between the two arms.

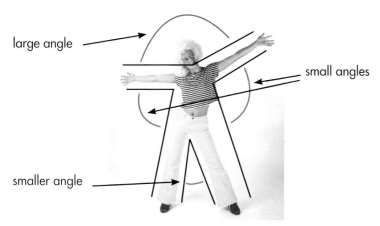

large angle

small angles

smaller angle

It does not matter how long each arm is. It does not matter in which direction the corner is facing. What matters is the amount of turn.

This is the symbol for an angle ∠

Sometimes only one arm is visible and you have to imagine the other arm such as when opening a door.

When the two arms are together at the start, there is no angle such as a closed door or the hands on a clock at 12 o'clock.

TURNS

Imagine you are standing in the middle of a circle. You can spin your body **clockwise** or **anti-clockwise**. You can turn a quarter of the way around, halfway around, three-quarters of the way around or all the way around. Angles measure how far you turn.

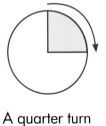
A quarter turn

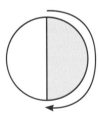
A half turn

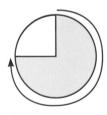
A three-quarter turn

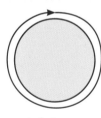
A full turn

Make your own angle maker.

Trace the rim of a plastic bottle onto different coloured pieces of cardboard.

Try this

Draw one straight line from the edge of your circles to the centre. Cut this line with scissors.

Fit the two circles together to create an angle maker. Practise creating $\frac{1}{4}$, $\frac{1}{2}$, $\frac{3}{4}$ and full turns.

You use angles when driving a car or a bike. The steering wheel needs to turn at just the right angle to get you where you want to go. Too small or too large an angle means you could have an accident.

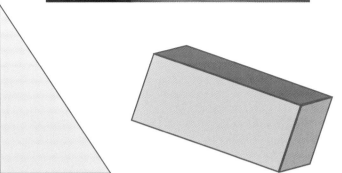

You can discover angles inside 2D shapes with straight sides.

You can discover angles on 3D shapes with flat faces.

TYPES OF ANGLES

Angles come in different sizes. Angle size is a measure of the amount of rotation.

You can sort angles in six different ways:

- acute
- right
- obtuse
- straight
- reflex
- full turn.

Do not get mixed up by all the different words. People love giving things special names. Once you know what each one looks like, you just need to picture it in your head.

RIGHT ANGLES

A quarter turn is called a **right angle**. The word 'right' comes from an old English word for straight. Perhaps because a right angle is where two straight lines are exactly a quarter turn apart.

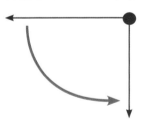

You say that the two lines on a right angle are **perpendicular**.

If an angle is a little bit larger or a little bit smaller than a right angle, then it is not a right angle. A right angle has to be exactly a quarter turn. In building or construction, everything is lopsided and messy if right angles are not measured exactly.

Sometimes angles look smaller or larger than a right angle even though they are right angles in real-life. Look carefully at photographs or drawings. Instead of looking at them from the side, imagine looking at the photograph from above.

MEASURING RIGHT ANGLES

Here are two geometric instruments that measure right angles. You place the right angle corner on top of the thing you are measuring. If it is exactly the same size, then it is a right angle.

This is the symbol for a right angle ⌐

Make your own right angle measurer.

Get a piece of paper and fold it in half. Fold this in half again. The folded corner is always a right angle.

Try this

ACUTE ANGLES

If the amount of turn between two straight lines is **less than a right angle**, you call it an **acute angle**. Even if the angle is just a tiny bit smaller than a right angle, it is still an acute angle.

Acute angles can face in any direction.

The length of the arms can be different.

But the angle must be smaller than a right angle.

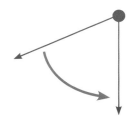

Try this

ACUTE ANGLES (continued)

Find three angles around you that are just a little bit smaller than a right angle.

Use your right angle measurer to check.

Every time you find an acute angle, imagine another acute angle beside it so that both are the same angle size as one right angle.

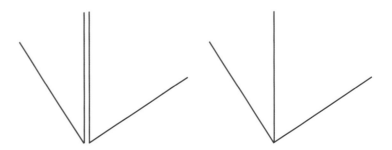

So every time you see one acute angle, you can imagine its right angle partner in your head.

Challenge

Can you find exactly two same-size acute angles that together measure one right angle?

Can you find exactly three same-size acute angles that together measure one right angle?

You can use different words to talk about acute angles. If a hill is gentle, then it is making a very small acute angle. If a hill is steep, then it is making quite a large acute angle.

A small door opening is called narrow. A larger door opening is called wide.

Look at this picture of a jumping girl.

How many acute angles can you find?

_____ acute angles

Try this

STRAIGHT ANGLES

A half turn is called a **straight angle**. That is because the two arms of the angle make a straight line. When you stretch out your two arms beside you, it is called a straight angle. This line can be in any direction.

These are all straight angles.

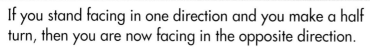

A straight angle is the same size as two quarter turns.

A straight angle is the same size as two right angles.

If you stand facing in one direction and you make a half turn, then you are now facing in the opposite direction.

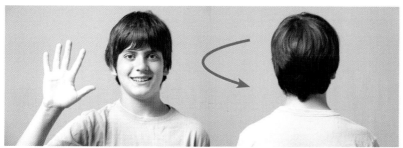

Make your own angle measurer using two strips of cardboard and a paper split pin.

You can now make any angle you like. Match this to any angle you want to measure. Press your fingers together so that you hold this angle. Find other angles in the room that are the same size as your angle.

Not all turning things can make a straight angle. Some doors cannot open this wide. Most scissors stop before you get a straight angle.

Try this

USING ANGLES

Angles are used in many games such as marbles, pinball or handball.

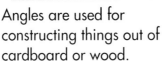

Angles are used in many sports such as soccer, minigolf or skiing.

Angles are used for constructing things out of cardboard or wood.

Angles are used in designing brick or tile patterns.

OBTUSE ANGLES

If the amount of turn is **more than a right angle but less than a straight angle**, you call it an **obtuse angle**. You can make a obtuse angle easily using your two arms or two legs.

These are all obtuse angles.

An obtuse angle is the same size as one right angle plus one acute angle.

If an angle is only a tiny bit larger than a right angle, then it is still an obtuse angle. If an angle is only a tiny bit smaller than a straight angle, then it is still an obtuse angle.

Find three angles, somewhere in your room, that are just a little bit larger than a right angle.

Use your right angle measurer to check.

Try this

REFLEX ANGLES

If the amount of turn is larger than a straight angle, then you call it a **reflex** angle. These are all reflex angles.

A reflex angle is the same size as one straight angle plus one acute, one right or one obtuse angle. These are all reflex angles.

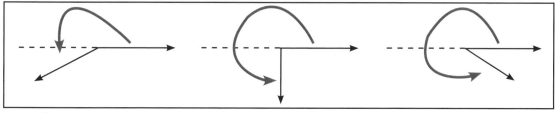

A reflex angle is larger than a straight angle but smaller than a full turn.

If an angle is only a tiny bit larger than a straight angle, then it is still a reflex angle. If an angle is only a tiny bit smaller than a full turn, then it is still a reflex angle.

FULL TURNS

A **full turn** makes the same shape as a circle.

It is the same size as four right angles.

It is the same size as two straight angles.

You see full circles in a clock, turning wheels on a bicycle or car, ice skaters and dancers when they spin on a point or the blades of a windmill turning with the wind.

Try this

How many different angles can you discover in this picture?

_____ angles

ANGLE SUMMARY

Name of angle	What the angle looks like
acute	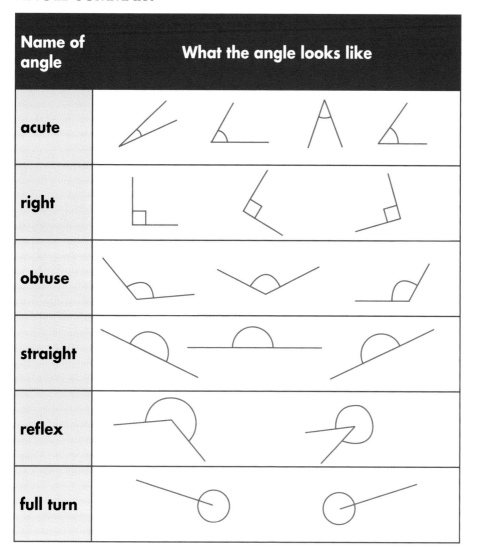
right	
obtuse	
straight	
reflex	
full turn	

Try this

Record the name of each angle you spot in these pictures.

LOCATING POSITIONS

SIMPLE MAPS

Every day of your life you are somewhere. Your body is located in the space around you. You are inside or outside. You are near your Gran's house or far away from it. You might live in the east part of town but south of the river.

Here are some words to help you talk about location.

right
along near
left up south
of north path street
east far in front
around above west down

A map is a way to record location. Maps are always drawn as a view from above, as if you are in a helicopter. You imagine looking down on the area.

Think of looking at your bed from above.

Try this

This is what it might look like on a map. →

You do not need to put in all the details.

You can write a label.

You can use symbols like this to show the location of selected objects.

| Bed |

Look at this drawing of a bedroom.

Try drawing it as a map viewed from above.

To explain to a friend how to walk from their house to your house you can sketch this as a simple map. Usually these maps are not to scale but include special landmarks.

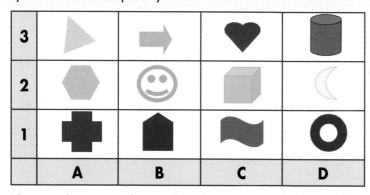

School

Smith Street

Your house

Shops

Red Avenue

Wattle Road

My house

Library

Look at this map.

Start at my house. Then explain to someone how to get to 'your house' using some of the location words on page 138.

CO-ORDINATES

Hundreds of years ago people worked out that a grid overlay makes map reading easier. Each space in the grid is named by letters or numbers called **co-ordinates**. This system was developed by a French man called Descartes.

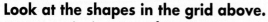

Try this

The purple cross is located in the square called A1. The pink prism is located in D3.

When reading co-ordinates, you say the horizontal grid name first, then the vertical grid name.

Look at the shapes in the grid above.
Try to say the location of each shape.

Try this

SCALE MAPS

Sometimes you need more details than a sketch map. You need all the street names, approximate distances and which direction to turn.

An accurate map can help you measure distances. When you use a grid overlay, a **scale** is used to help you know the size of everything.

Scale: 1 cm on the grid might represent 10 metres in real life.

A map **legend** tells you what the symbols on your map mean.

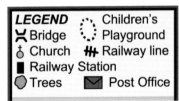

LEGEND
⋈ Bridge   ⬭ Children's Playground
♁ Church   ╫ Railway line
■ Railway Station
⬡ Trees   ✉ Post Office

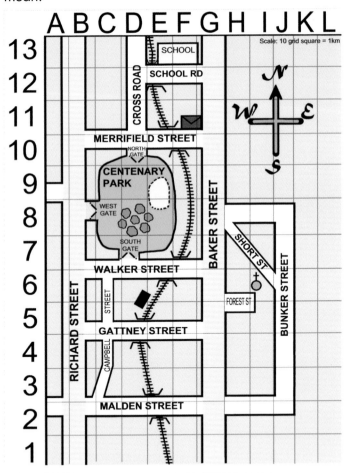

Use this street map to write the co-ordinate reference for each place:

1 Train station
2 Church
3 School
4 Playground
5 Walker Street bridge
6 Post Office

FOUR COMPASS POINTS

Our 3D earth rotates from west to east each day.

To us it looks like the sun rises in the east but really it is just our earth moving towards the east. This movement creates our four main directions, the **cardinal points**:

North
East
South
West

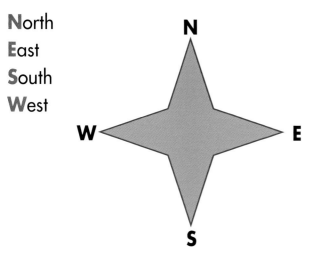

Compasses were first invented at least 700 years ago possibly by the Chinese using a magnetised needle.

Imagine these points as a 2D circle where they rotate in a clockwise direction starting at North. You can record them using just the capital letter at the start of each word **N E S W**.

Maps show where north is with an arrow. You need to look carefully as not all maps are drawn with N located at the top of the page.

N

The cardinal points are called compass points because you can use a compass to find out which direction you are facing such as when you are bushwalking.

A compass is designed to always point north.

FOUR COMPASS POINTS (continued)

You can be a human compass and face north.

Go outside and see where the sun is in the morning. This is east. If you stand with east on your right, then you are looking north.

Check again in the afternoon. The sun should now be in the west. Stand with the sun on your left and you should be again looking north. South is behind you.

Try this

Some people place a NESW weathervane on the top of their house. This shows the direction of the wind.

Challenge

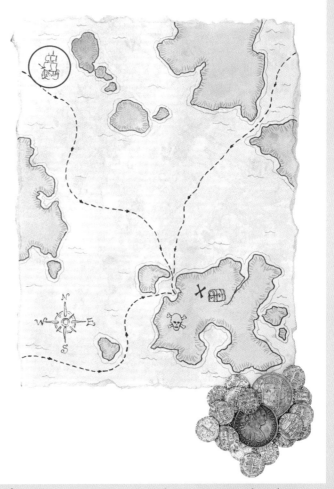

Look at this map showing where treasure has been buried. Give directions to the ship's captain so that you reach the treasure safely. Use north, south, east and west in your directions.

EIGHT COMPASS POINTS

The North, South, East and West compass points can also be divided into four more compass directions.

- Halfway between North and East is Northeast – NE.
  You keep rotating clockwise.
- Southeast is halfway between East and South – SE.
- Southwest is halfway between South and West – SW.
- Northwest is halfway between West and North – NW.

Use these eight compass points to describe and identify directions more accurately.

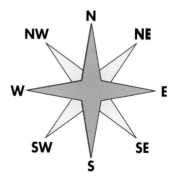

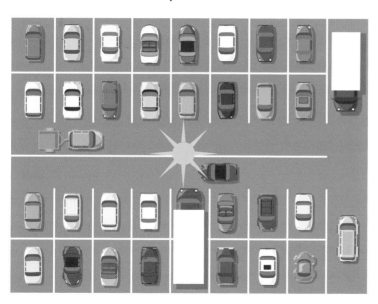

Look at this map of a carpark.

If you stand on the facing N:

- a yellow car is to the NW
- a blue and a green car are directly N
- a purple car is to your NE
- a white car is to your SW.

EIGHT COMPASS POINTS (continued)

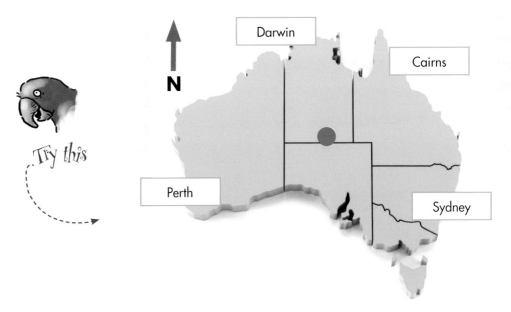

Try this

Look at this map of Australia.

If you lived at the centre, marked ●, in which direction are each of the marked cities located?

Challenge

Look at this circular map.

- The striped lighthouse is SE of the ship.

- The yellow car is N of the whale.

- The green mountains are NW of the yellow house.

Find five more objects to locate using the eight compass points. Write your directions.

CHANCE

The African Stone Game or Mankala has been played for over 1300 years. It is the oldest game of chance in the world.

Chance is about whether something will or will not happen. It is about having two or more choices such as:

- winning or not winning a game

- visiting or not visiting your cousin

- wearing your red shorts or your blue ones.

CHANCE GAMES

Chance games are fair if you and a partner have an equal chance of winning. If the result is **random**, then you say you are lucky if you win or unlucky if you lose.

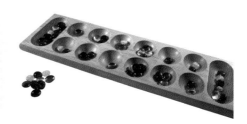

Random results happen when you:

play a board game	toss a coin	draw a coloured ball out of a bag

turn over a card	rotate a spinner	throw some dice

 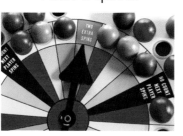 

CHANCE GAMES (continued)

Here are some words to help you talk about chance.

impossible
certain **predict** **unsure** **could**
possible **likely** **probably**
unfair
might **random** **unlikely**

It is possible for an elephant to stand on a ball but impossible for it to grow wings and fly.

If the result is uncertain, then it is a chance event.

- You win the competition or you don't.
- You win the lottery or you don't.

If the result is certain, then it is not a chance event.

- If the balls in a bag are all blue, then you can only pull out a blue ball.
- If today is Monday, then tomorrow must be Tuesday.

TWO-RESULT EVENTS

Some people believe in fortune tellers who think they can predict the future. Sometimes what they say is true and sometimes it is untrue. It is a chance event. A **prediction** is where you say what you think will happen before it does.

Coin toss

When you toss a coin, there are only two possibilities.

heads (H) or tails (T)

There is a 1 in 2 chance of getting heads.

If you toss the coin 10 times, you expect or predict 5 H and 5 T. But as it is a chance event, your prediction is not always correct. By chance you might get 8 H and 2 T.

The more times you toss a coin, the more chance you have of getting closer to your prediction. Tossing the coin 10 times is a very small **sample**. Even a sample of 20 or 50 tosses is small. Some people like to try 100 or more times. Some people try over 1000 times.

Throw a dice

When you throw a six-sided dice, there are six possible numbers.

The number shown could be odd or even. Both events have an equal chance.

- Three out of six or $\frac{3}{6}$ throws could score a 1, 3 or 5. This is a 1 in 2 chance.
- Three out of six or $\frac{3}{6}$ throws could score a 2, 4 or 6. This is another 1 in 2 chance.

Balls in a bag

Red or Blue

Put 1 red ball and 1 blue ball in a bag. If you take one ball out without looking, then it will be either red or blue. There is a one in two chance it is red. There is a 1 in 2 chance it will be blue. It is an equal chance. It is fair.

If there are 10 red balls in the bag, how many blue balls do you need inside the bag to keep it an equal chance?

_____ blue balls

Try this

TWO-RESULT EVENTS (continued)

Pack of cards

In a pack of 52 playing cards, half are red cards and half are black cards.

Red or black

Try this

Shuffle a pack of playing cards and place them face down. Predict whether the top card will be red or black when you turn it over. Record your prediction. Record the actual result.

What chance do you have of getting red?

Is this a fair chance? Why?

UNEQUAL CHANCES

If a chance event has two outcomes, or results, it does not mean it always has an equal chance of happening.

Throw two dice

If you throw two dice, then both numbers can be the same (doubles). Both numbers can be different. If you list all possibilities, you can see there are 36 possible outcomes.

Possible dice pairs (with doubles in red)

	1	2	3	4	5	6
1	(11)	12	13	14	15	16
2	21	(22)	23	24	25	26
3	31	32	(33)	34	35	36
4	41	42	43	(44)	45	46
5	51	52	53	54	(55)	56
6	61	62	63	64	65	(66)

You have only six chances of getting doubles.

Six out of thirty-six,

$\frac{6}{36}$

1 in 6 chance

You have 30 chances of not getting doubles.

Thirty out of thirty-six

$\frac{30}{36}$

5 in 6 chance

It is an unequal chance for throwing doubles. It is not a fair chance.

Balls in a bag

If you have 1 red ball (R) and 4 blue balls (B) in a bag and you put your hand in and draw one out, then it will be either red or blue.

- There are five possible outcomes – R, B, B, B, B.
- You have 1 in 5 chances, or $\frac{1}{5}$, it will be red.
- You have 4 in 5 chances, or $\frac{4}{5}$, it will be blue.
- It is an unequal chance. It is not fair.

Try this

You have 10 balls in a bag. One is red, the others are black.

1 What chance do you have of drawing out a red ball?

2 What chance do you have of drawing out a black ball?

3 Is it a fair chance?

RANDOM EVENTS

Some people think that if one event has happened, then it probably will not happen again for a while. This is not true.

Roy Sullivan was struck by lightning 7 times over 35 years.

Spinners

A two-colour spinner can stop at any colour. Just because it stopped last time at yellow, it does not mean it cannot stop at yellow again.

Babies

A baby can be either a girl or a boy. Just because mum had a baby boy last time, it does not mean she will have a girl this time.

Balls under a cup

Just because the ball was in the middle last time, it does not mean it will be somewhere else next time.

ORDERING CHANCE EVENTS

You can label chance events according to their **probability**. Probability is about describing the chance or likelihood that something will happen.

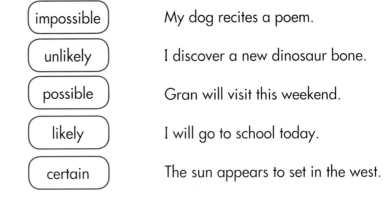

impossible	My dog recites a poem.
unlikely	I discover a new dinosaur bone.
possible	Gran will visit this weekend.
likely	I will go to school today.
certain	The sun appears to set in the west.

You can put chance events in order from impossible to certain. Use proportional reasoning to help you do this.

Try this

Write these chance words in one of the 5 columns.

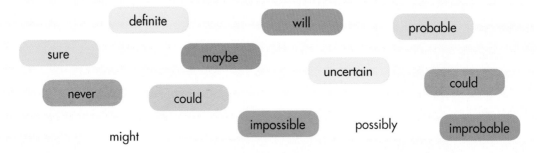

definite   will   probable

sure   maybe   uncertain

never   could   could

might   impossible   possibly   improbable

No Chance	Unlikely	Even chance	Likely	Certain

DATA DISPLAYS

Data is all about asking a question and then collecting answers so that you can analyse, talk about and explain your results. **Statistics** is a way of thinking about what the numbers mean.

ASKING QUESTIONS

What sort of questions do you ask? This is totally up to you. What would you like to know? Once you have your question, you need to find a way to record what you count. A **table** helps you organise your data so you can keep track of your results.

You can conduct a simple survey by asking 10 people whether they prefer dogs or cats. There are only two possible answers – dogs or cats. Tally the results from 10 people and see what you discover.

Tally marks help you skip count by 5s.

I prefer dogs	I prefer cats
ⲧⲏⲏⲧ 1	111

You now have some statistics that allow you to make statements such as 'more people like dogs than cats' or 'fewer people like cats'.

Other questions you might like to investigate are:

Do you prefer vegemite or salad sandwiches?

Vegemite	Salad

Which is your favourite meal – breakfast, lunch or dinner?

Data questions could also survey the number of vehicles that go past your house every hour, the top 10 products sold in a supermarket or the number of TV programs that are for children.

Breakfast	Lunch	Dinner

Every five years the Australian Bureau of Statistics (ABS) conducts a census. They ask every household to fill out a detailed survey. A household means you count every person living in that house. The results help the Government plan so they know exactly when and where they need to build new hospitals, schools or roads.

Try this

SAMPLE SIZE

A **sample** is where you collect data from only some members of a group.

A **census** is where you collect data from every single person in the group.

The smallest sample would be two people. You cannot say much about the results with two people. If you like vegemite and I like salad, then 'half the people like vegemite' is not a fair statement. The sample size is too small. Statistics is used in advertisements. When you read these advertisements, you need to remember that if the advertiser used a very small sample, then what they say is misleading.

You need to collect opinions from more people to get better statistics. Remember that statistics is about numbers. The more numbers you collect, the more accurate are your statements.

You can be absolutely sure of your facts when you conduct a census. If you asked everyone in your school the 'Do you prefer dogs or cats?' survey, then you would know for sure which pet was the most popular at your school.

Use this data from a recent ABS Census to make at least three statements about Australian households.

Number of households with home internet	Average amount spent on food in a week	Average amount spent on transport in a week	Number of people in NSW	Number of people in SA	Number of people born in 1 year	Number of deaths in 1 year
7 234 560	$153	$139	7 253 400	1 647 800	301 500	141 700

TWO-WAY TABLES

Once you understand how to ask questions and conduct a simple survey to match, you can try collecting data using a two-way table. This time you ask a question but record the answers from two different types of people.

For example, you might ask 30 classmates: 'Do you prefer dogs or cats?' But this time you record whether you ask a girl (variable 1) or a boy (variable 2). To make it fair, you can ask 15 girls and 15 boys.

Type of person	I prefer dogs	I prefer cats
Girl	⁀卌 II	卌 III
Boy	卌 卌 I	IIII

Analyse the data, then use your statistics to make statements such as 'about half of the girls prefer dogs' or 'more girls than boys like cats' or '11 out of 15 boys liked dogs'.

Try this

Ask every person in your family to do this two-way hat survey.

Which hat do they think is the funniest?

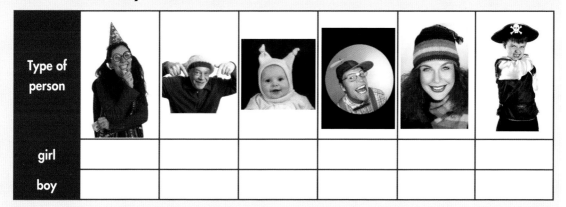

Type of person						
girl						
boy						

1 The most popular hat is _____

2 The least popular hat is _____

3 More girls than boys like _____

4 More boys than girls like _____

GRAPHS

Once you collect data, you can display your results in a graph. A graph helps you see things differently. Some people find it easier to look at a graph than to read information in a list or a table. A graph is more visual.

There are many types of graphs. You need to choose the one you think best displays what you discovered.

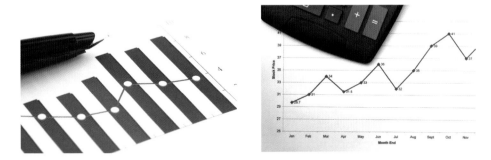

ONE-TO-ONE PICTURE GRAPHS

Draw or cut out one picture for every fact collected. The lines of pictures can be horizontal → or vertical ↑.

Food we prefer to eat

This 'Food we prefer to eat' graph has pictures placed unequally. It is not a good graph. The row of vegetable pictures is the same length as the row of meat pictures but more people liked vegetables.

Try to keep all the pictures neat and tidy and similar sizes. You should have the pictures in neat rows and columns. If you imagine grid lines, then it is easy to see which food is the most popular.

This is a better way to make a picture graph:

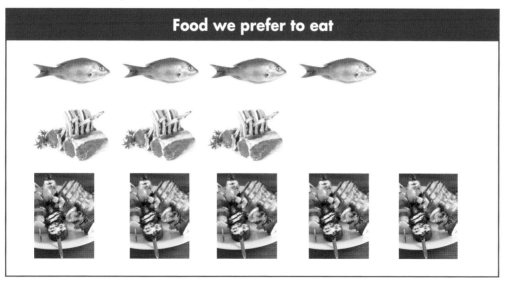

Food we prefer to eat

You now analyse your data and find statistical things to say like 'vegetables are the most popular food', 'more people chose fish than meat' or 'the second most popular food was fish'.

Always give your graph a name or title. This describes what your graph is about. You can also use a geometric symbol to save having to draw details.

Our Favourite Footwear	
Thongs	~~ЖЖ~~ 11
Shoes	11
Joggers	~~ЖЖ~~

Our Favourite Footwear							
Thongs	●	●	●	●	●	●	●
Shoes	●	●					
Joggers	●	●	●	●	●		

You now analyse your data and find statistical things to say like '14 people were surveyed' or 'shoes were the least popular footwear' or 'only 2 people chose shoes'.

MANY-TO-ONE GRAPHS

One space for every fact works well for a small sample. But what if you collect 100 or more facts? Your graph will be too long or too high. You will run out of room on your page.

Look at this object graph. It shows how many biscuits were baked at Jan's Bakery over three days. Each biscuit represents 100 biscuits.

Jan's Daily Biscuit Graph

| Monday | Tuesday | Wednesday |

Scale: One biscuit represents 100 biscuits

On Monday, there were 3 × 100 biscuits baked. That's 300 biscuits.

On Tuesday, there were 5 × 100 biscuits baked. That's 500 biscuits.

Look at Jan's Daily Biscuit Graph.

How many biscuits were baked on Wednesday?

_____ biscuits

Try this

Challenge

How many biscuits did Jan bake altogether from Monday to Wednesday?

_____ biscuits

So each space in a graph can represent more than one fact.

You can make your own scale.

For example, 1 space = 10 facts

Our Favourite Footwear							
Thongs	●	●	●	●	●	●	●
Shoes	●	●					
Joggers	●	●	●	●	●		

Scale = 10

Even though this graph looks the same as the earlier one, there are now 14 × 10 facts collected. That's 140 facts.

70 people have chosen thongs, not 7 people.

Your statistics will be more accurate with 140 in the sample size.

Try this

Look at the 'Our Favourite Footwear' graph.

1 If your scale is ● = 2, how many people like thongs?

2 If your scale is ● = 5, how many people like shoes?

3 If your scale is ● = 20, how many people like joggers?

COLUMN GRAPHS

Instead of pictures or symbols, in a column graph, you use a space on a grid to represent each fact you collect. The columns can be horizontal → or vertical ↑.

You need:

- a name for the horizontal facts
- a name for the vertical facts (this name tells what the spaces represent)
- a name for your graph.

COLUMN GRAPHS (continued)

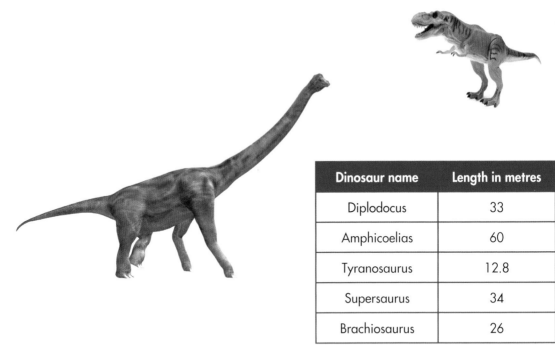

Dinosaur name	Length in metres
Diplodocus	33
Amphicoelias	60
Tyranosaurus	12.8
Supersaurus	34
Brachiosaurus	26

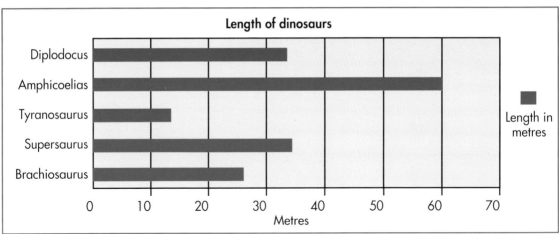

Notice that only the vertical grid lines are drawn on this graph. The horizontal lines are invisible. Sometimes all the grid lines on a column graph are invisible. But you still need the numbered marks on the side to tell you what each space represents.

Notice that the horizontal axis spaces are scaled to 10 m apart. You use proportional reasoning to mark these or you can use a ruler.

You now analyse your data and find statistical things to say like 'These dinosaurs are all longer than 10 metres' or '4 of these dinosaurs are longer than 20 m'.

The same data looks like this in a vertical column graph.

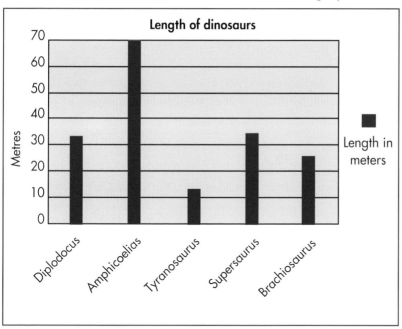

Length of dinosaurs

Try this

Analyse the data in this two-way table.

I am the heaviest fish

World's 10 Heaviest Fish

Name of fish	Maximum mass in kilograms	Maximum length in metres	Maximum age in years
Whale shark	11800	12.65	70
Basking shark	5218	12.27	
Great white shark	2268	6	30
Ocean sunfish	1000	3.2	10
Giant Cambodian stingray	455	4.3	
Pirarucu	180	2.5	
Mekong giant catfish	300	3.2	
Beluga sturgeon	264	6	118
Bull shark	250	3.5	
Wels catfish	150	3	

Make three statistical statements about what you discover.

SYMBOLS & ABBREVIATIONS

Number

=	equal
+	plus
–	minus
×	multiply
÷	divide
<	less than
>	more than

Length

mm	millimetre
cm	centimetre
m	metre

10 mm = 1 cm

100 cm = 1 m

Area

m^2	square metre
cm^2	square centimetre
mm^2	square millimetre

Volume and capacity

m^3	cubic metre
cm^3	cubic centimetre
L	litre
mL	millilitre

Mass

g	gram
kg	kilogram

Time

h	hour
min	minute
s	second
am	before midday (ante meridiem)
pm	after midday (post meridiem)

Space

2D	Two dimensional
3D	Three dimensional

Temperature

°C	degrees Celsius

Angles

∠ angle

⌐ right angle

SELECTED TRY THIS AND CHALLENGE ANSWERS

NUMBER & ALGEBRA

Page 1   **Even numbers**
1 42, 58,
2 104, 476, 702
3 1098, 3974, 7030

Page 2   **Odd numbers**
1 51, 77, 93
2 695, 849
3 3999, 8833

Page 4   **Tens and ones**
54 paperclips

Page 5   **Hundreds**
1 528
2 258
3 582

Page 7   **Thousands**
1 3490
2 9430
3 4930
4 4093

Page 8   **Ten thousand**
$982

Page 9   **Ten thousand**
1 1001 L
2 $5999
3 17 055 kg
4 10 401 m
1 $8712
2 37 055 m

Page 9   **Place value names**
1 56 000
2 572
3 1500
4 15 366

Page 11   **Adding and subtracting fact family**
Set 1 15, 8, 19, 14, 9, 11, 7, 8, 8, 11
Set 2 9, 10, 8, 4, 5, 5, 6, 4, 3, 6
1 313, 2013
2 507, 3007

Page 13   **Adding and subtracting multiples of 10**
Table 1 70, 80, 100, 120, 100, 190, 120, 150, 110, 140
Table 2 50, 20, 60, 30, 30, 30, 60, 70, 90, 70
Table 3 5, 2, 6, 9, 3, 9, 7, 4
Challenge 860

Page 14   **Adding and subtracting multiples of 10**
73, 68, 99, 85, 85, 174, 138, 132, 128, 145

Page 14   **Adding and subtracting multiples of 10**
58, 27, 32, 11, 64, 85, 77, 86, 48, 99

Page 15   **Adding pairs to 100**
1 58 cm
2 47 mL
3 29 g
4 12 m^2

Page 16   **Adding any two-digit numbers**
1 $88
2 $103
3 $109
4 $180

Page 16   **Doubling any two-digit numbers**
1 70
2 144
3 172
4 188
Challenge 1020

Page 17   **Halving any two-digit number**
1 $14\frac{1}{2}$
2 $36\frac{1}{2}$
3 44
4 $49\frac{1}{2}$
Challenge 410

Page 21   **Groups of 2**
1 18 feet
2 20 eyes
3 14 legs 4 16 L
Challenge $56

Page 23   **Groups of 5**
1 $30
2 25
3 50
4 30 m
Challenge 90

Page 25   **Groups of 10**
1 $80
2 40
3 90
Challenge 180

Page 34   **Times table grid**
The rows also show multiples of the number at the left of the row; the main diagonal from top left to bottom right shows square numbers
Challenge 200, 560

Page 36 Fraction language

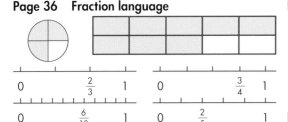

| 0 | $\frac{2}{3}$ | 1 | 0 | $\frac{3}{4}$ | 1 |

| 0 | $\frac{6}{10}$ | 1 | 0 | $\frac{2}{5}$ | 1 |

Page 39 Halves, quarters and eighths
1 $\frac{1}{4}$
2 $\frac{4}{8}$ or $\frac{2}{4}$ **3** $\frac{2}{2}$ or $\frac{8}{8}$

Page 43 Ordering decimals
1 6.1
2 1.0
3 2
4 32.1

Page 48 $5, $10, $20, $50 and $100 notes
$3.85
Challenge **1** 915
2 457 plus 5 c
3 228 plus 10 c and 5 c
4 91 plus 20 c and 5 c

Page 50 Number sentences
6 × 7 + 3 = 45

Page 52 Creating a pattern rule

Step 5	(5 x 5) + 5	25 + 5	30
Step 6	(6 x 6) + 6	36 + 6	42
Step 7	(7 x 7) + 7	49 + 7	56

MEASUREMENT & GEOMETRY
Page 61 Tips about measuring length
2950 mm, 295 cm

Page 73 Ordering masses
750 g, 1100 g, 1.45 kg

Page 79 Measuring volume by counting cubes
12 cubes, 16 cubes, 8 cubes
Challenge: 48 cubes

Page 86 Analogue clocks
3 o'clock, 7 o'clock, 11 o'clock, 12 o'clock, 4 o'clock, 9 o'clock
1:30, 4:30, 9:30

Page 87 Analogue clocks
3:15, 7:15, 11:15

Page 88 Analogue clocks
2:45, 8:45, 12:45
1:25, 4:42, 10:56

Page 89 Digital clocks
nine thirty-five, 9:35,
25 minutes to 10

Page 90 Solving time problems
1 $1\frac{1}{2}$ hours
2 185 minutes
3 131

Page 91 Calendar
1 30
2 5
3 3 April
4 Saturday 16 April
5 Sunday 24 April
6 15 April

Page 94 Temperature
1 170 °C
2 39 °C
3 –10 °C
4 0 °C

Page 96 Weather forecasts
Challenge 74 °C, 41 °C, 26 °C, 28 °C, 25 °C, 22 °C, 38 °C, 34 °C, 15 °C

Page 114 Straight line facts
There are many horizontal, vertical, parallel, perpendicular and oblique lines. How many of each did you discover?

Page 125 Symmetry

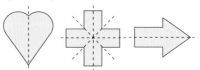

Page 137 Angle summary
clock has a reflex, obtuse and reflex angles
soccer ball has obtuse angles
box has right angles

Page 140 Scale maps
1 D6
2 I6
3 F13
4 E9
5 E7
6 F11

Page 144 Eight compass points
Perth is SW, Darwin is NW, Cairns is NE, Sydney is SE

STATISTICS & PROBABILITY
Page 147 Two-result events
10 blue balls

Page 149 Unequal chances
1 1 in 10 chance
2 9 out of 10 chance
3 it is not a fair chance as there are many more black balls

Page 156 Many-to-one graphs
800 biscuits

Page 157 Many-to-one graphs
1 14 people **2** 10 people **3** 100 people

GLOSSARY

acute angle	Any angle less than a right angle
addition	The operation of combining two or more numbers to find the total
analogue clock	A clock or watch with a circular face numbered from 1 to 12 or 1 to 24, showing time as the angle between two rotating hands
anti-clockwise	Circular movement in the opposite direction to the hands on an analogue clock
apex	This is the highest point, vertex or pointy end of an object
array	A grid system of rows and columns for sorting objects into equal groups
average	The number you get when you add two or more sets of numbers and divide by the number of sets
base 10	A place value number system based on groups of 10 using the digits 0 to 9
calibrations	Small marks on a measuring device showing precise measurements between two larger measurements
capacity	A measure of how much a container can hold, measured in litres, millilitres and kilolitres
cardinal points	The four main directions of North (N), South (S), East (E) and West (W)
census	A data collection system where you collect information from every person in the group
centimetre	A small unit of length equal to one hundredth of a metre
circle	A special curved 2D shape that has only one side, with each point along the side, or circumference, exactly the same distance from the centre
circumference	The length around the outside of a circle, where every point is exactly the same distance from the centre
clockwise	Circular movement in the same direction as the hands on an analogue clock
cone	A 3D solid with one circular face and one curved surface that ends in a point or vertex
co-ordinates	A grid system of rows and columns that helps you identify position using different numbers or letters to refer to each space in the grid
cross-section	The 2D shape you get when you cut a slice straight through any 3D object
cube	A square prism or regular hexahedron, with 6 square faces, 8 vertices and 12 edges
cubic centimetre	A very small 3D unit of volume or capacity that measures 1 cm × 1 cm × 1 cm
cubic metre	A large 3D unit of volume and capacity that measures 1 m × 1 m × 1 m
cubical	A way to describe any 3D solid that looks like a cube
curved surface	The outside layer of the curved part of a 3D object such as a cylinder, cone or sphere
cylinder	A 3D solid with two identical circular faces at either end of one curved surface
cylindrical	A way to describe any 3D solid that looks like a cylinder

date	A system for measuring time in days, months and years
decimal point	The symbol used to separate the whole number from the decimal fraction
degrees Celsius	The unit for measuring temperature where 0° C equals the freezing point of pure water and 100° C represents the boiling point of pure water at standard pressure
denominator	The bottom number in a fraction or the total number of equal parts into which something has been divided
diagonal	Any straight line joining two opposite corners of a rectangle or other polygons with five or more sides
difference	The result in a subtraction problem when you find the amount by which one number is larger or smaller than another number
digital clock	A device for measuring and displaying time as numbers from 0:00 to either 11:59 (12 hour time) or 23:59 (24 hour time)
digits	The ten symbols from 0–9 used to record any number in the base 10 number system
division	The operation of putting things into equal groups or sharing equally by repeated subtraction
edge	The line on a 3D solid where two faces meet
equilateral triangle	A regular polygon with three identical length straight sides and three identical angles
equivalent fractions	Different ways to describe the same fractional part of an object even though the numerators and denominators are different
even number	A whole number that can be put into pairs or groups of two, with no left overs
face	Any flat 2D surface on a 3D solid
factor	Each of the two whole numbers that multiply to create a product or a number that divides equally into another larger number
fifths	Five same-size fractions created by dividing something into five equal parts
flip	The action of repeating a 2D shape to a new position on the opposite side of a line of symmetry, also called reflection
gram	A small unit for measuring the mass or heaviness of an object
halves	Two same-size fractions created by dividing something into two equal parts
heft	Estimate the mass of an object or how heavy something feels by holding it in your hands
hemisphere	Half a sphere
horizontal line	A straight line that goes from left to right like the horizon and is parallel to the ground
hour	A unit of time where one day is divided into 24 equal parts from midnight onwards until the next midnight
hundreds	A three-digit number in the base 10 decimal place value system representing groups of 10 × 10, including any number from 100 to 999 is in the hundreds
hundreds place	The number in the third position from the right in any whole number equal to or larger than 100

hundredths	One hundred same-size fractions created by dividing something up into 100 equal parts
kilogram	A metric unit for measuring mass or the heaviness of an object, where 1000 grams is the same as one kilogram
legend	This shows you what the symbols on a map represent in real-life
line of symmetry	A straight line through a shape where both sides perfectly reflect at every point along the line, cutting the shape into two matching halves
litre	A unit for measuring volume and capacity based on a 10 cm x 10 cm x 10 cm cube
maximum	The largest possible number in a given event such as the highest temperature in one day
metre	The base unit for measuring length where 1 metre equals 100 centimetres or 1000 millimetres
midday	The middle of a 24-hour day when the sun is high up in the sky, 12 hours after midnight, 12:00 or noon
midnight	The end of a 24-hour day in the middle of the night and then the new day's cycle starts immediately after midnight
millilitre	A very small 3D metric unit for measuring volume and capacity where 1000 mL is the same as one litre
millimetre	A very small unit of length where 10 mm is the same as one centimetre
minimum	The smallest possible number in a given event, such as the lowest temperature in one day
minus	Another name for take away or subtract, when you find the difference between two numbers. In temperature a minus number is less than 0° Celsius.
minute	A small unit of time where one hour is divided into 60 equal parts where 60 minutes is the same as one hour
multiple	The result when the same number is added continuously or the product of a particular number and any other whole number
multiplication	The operation of repeatedly adding the same number to get a product
net	A flat 2D shape that can be cut out and folded to make a 3D solid
numerator	The top number in a fraction, the selected number of equal parts
oblique line	A straight line that is slanting to the left or the right
obtuse angle	Any angle more than a right angle but less than a straight angle
odd number	A whole number that has one left over when you put it into pairs or groups of 2
ones	Another name for units in the base 10 decimal place value system, and whole numbers smaller than 10 and any leftover numbers from counting out a group of 10
ones place	The number in the first position from the right in any whole number
parallel line	Two or more straight lines that are exactly the same distance apart at every point along their lengths where they never touch or cross over each other
perimeter	The total length around the outside of any 2D shape
perpendicular lines	Two lines that meet at a right angle

place value	This is the base 10 value a digit represents in specific positions in a number such as the 3 representing three thousands in 3496
polygon	Any 2D shape with three or more straight sides and three or more angles
powers of 10	Numbers that are formed by multiplying 10 by 10 many times
prediction	Where you say what you think will happen before it does
prism	A 3D solid with two identical flat faces, or bases, at either end, joined by rectangles or parallelograms
probability	This is a way of describing how likely it is that a chance event will happen
product	The result in a multiplication problem when you multiply two or more numbers together
quadrilateral	Any 2D shape with four straight sides and four angles where a square is the only regular quadrilateral
quarters	Four same-size fractions created by dividing something up into four equal parts called fourths
quotient	The answer in a division problem when you divide one number by another number
random	If a result in a chance event is random, it is unknown and unpredictable
range	The difference between the highest and lowest numbers, for example the difference between the highest and lowest temperatures for one day
rays	Any two straight lines that meet at a point to create an angle
reflex angle	Any angle more than a straight angle but less than a full turn
reflection	An identical copy, or mirror image, of a design that has been flipped along the opposite side of a line of symmetry
regular hexahedron	This is a square prism or a cube where all six square faces are identical
regular polygon	Any straight-sided 2D shape where every side is exactly the same length and every angle is the same size
regular 3D solid	A 3D solid with identical shaped faces and equal length edges such as tetrahedron, cube, octahedron, dodecahedron, icosahedron
right angle	Any angle that is exactly a quarter turn
sample	This is where you collect information from a selected group of actions. You do not collect every possible result
scale	When you use a grid overlay on a reduced size map or drawing, the scale tells you how to interpret the reduced proportions such as 1 cm on a map might represent 1 km in real-life
second	A very small unit of time where one minute is divided into 60 equal parts where 60 seconds is the same as one minute
skeleton model	A see-through 3D model where you see just the edges and vertices and not the faces of a 3D object
skip count	To count by numbers other than one
sphere	A special 3D solid that has one curved surface only, shaped like a ball
square centimetre	A small 2D metric unit of area covering 1 cm x 1 cm
square metre	A 2D metric unit of area covering 1 m x 1 m
statistics	A system where you collect, classify, analyse and interpret information in relation to probability

straight angle	Any angle that is exactly two right angles or half a full turn
subtraction	The operation of finding the difference between two sets of numbers
sum	The total in an addition problem when two or more numbers are added
surface area	The total area of the surface of a 3D shape
symmetrical	Any shape that has at least one line of symmetry or one mirror line, where one half of the shape is perfectly reflected in the other half
table	A grid system of rows and columns to help you organise information and keep track of your results
temperature	A measure of how hot or cold something is using a thermometer to measure in degrees Celsius
tens of thousands	A five-digit number in the base 10 decimal place value system representing groups of $10 \times 10 \times 10 \times 10$ where any number from 10 000 to 99 999 is in the ten thousands
tens of thousands place	The number in the fifth position from the right in any whole number equal to or larger than 10 000
tens	A two-digit number in the base 10 decimal place value system representing groups of 10 where any number from 10 to 99 is in the tens
tens place	The number in the second position from the right in any whole number equal to or larger than 10
tenths	Ten same-size fractions created by dividing something into 10 equal parts
tessellate	The action of fitting 2D shapes together so that there are no gaps and no overlaps
tetrahedron	Another name for a triangular pyramid
thermometer	A device for measuring temperature, or how hot or cold something is, using small units called degrees Celsius
thousands	A four-digit number in the base 10 decimal place value system representing groups of $10 \times 10 \times 10$ where any number from 1000 to 9999 is in the thousands
thousands place	The number in the fourth position from the right in any whole number equal to or larger than 1000
triangular prism	A 3D solid with two triangular bases at opposite ends, joined by three rectangular faces
units	The specific, identical measurements used in length, area, mass, volume and capacity, and time
vertex	The point where two or more straight lines meet to create a corner
vertical lines	Straight lines that are in an up and down position, perpendicular to the ground
vertices	The plural of vertex, used when there are two or more points
vinculum	The line, or fraction bar, that separates the numerator from the denominator
volume	A measure of how much 3D space an object takes up, measured in cm^3, m^3, L and mL

INDEX